THE EUCHARIST
AND
THE TRINITY

M.V. BERNADOT, O.P.

Michael Glazier, Inc.

Translation copyright © by Michael Glazier, Inc.
Library of Congress catalog card number - 77-7730
ISBN 0-89453-072-0

This work was originally published by Sands & Co. Ltd., London, under the title *From Holy Communion to the Holy Trinity*.

This edition with a revised translation, first published 1977 by Michael Glazier, Inc., 1210 A King Street, Wilmington, Delaware 19801. Printed in the United States.

PUBLISHER'S NOTE

There are some books that profoundly influence our lives. Perhaps we read them many years ago; possibly, they are long forgotten by all but ourselves. But, they still haunt us. More than two decades have passed since I read this small work. And over the years I have remembered it, even though I didn't re-read it until quite recently. I realized then that a mere appreciation of a spiritual challenge is not a response to it. The latter is the heart of the matter.

The author, M. V. Bernadot, O. P., was gifted with extraordinary insight and foresight. He founded and was the first editor of *La Vie Spirituelle* which was, and still is, the most influential and formative journal of spirituality in the history of the Church. This is a bold claim. But, I doubt that even a few would argue with it. Here was a man of vast vision who walked and worked in the presence of the living God. He was a man of rare spiritual sensitivity, a holy man, a man concerned.

When he wrote this book, Bernadot was pastorally concerned. He felt that the wonders of our faith were submerged by rotes and rules and regulations, which were originally formulated to help us appreciate these wonders. However, sadly and in a very real sense, they accomplished the exact opposite: we lost the gift and kept the wrapping. This work returns the gift.

I have always thought this was a spiritual classic. I didn't know if more competent people shared my view. So, I contacted a learned friend, Austin Flannery, O.P., the distinguished editor of *Doctrine and Life*, and he confirmed my hunch. Among his immediate confreres, he found two who cherished it as a book to have and to hold and to re-read again and again.

The original translator of this work, Dom Francis Izard, O.S.B., was a brilliant theologian, who recognized and cherished its doctrinal grandeur and perennial pertinence. He viewed it as a simple, yet profound, book which should be read by generations of Christians yet unborn—because its theme is timeless, its doctrine dateless. However while the original translation was literally exact, it was turgid and archaic in many ways. So it was deemed wise to have it completely re-written, and the task was splendidly performed by Penny Livermore.

You hold a spiritual classic in your hands.

Michael Glazier
1977

CONTENTS

VI
THE END OF THE EUCHARISTIC UNION

I. THE PURPOSE OF THIS BOOK

By the grace of God, many people are receiving Holy Communion daily at the present time.

These are good people who love Our Lord and approach the Communion rail with the intention desired by the Church. Yet, experience teaches us that something is lacking. It shows us clearly that they do not benefit as deeply as they should from this frequent reception of such a beautiful Sacrament.

What *is* lacking? Simply this: most people do not sufficiently grasp the eucharistic mystery and the marvellous reality of Holy Communion. And so, this little book is addressed to these Christians "of good will" in hopes that it may help them by enlightening their minds with greater knowledge. We wish to help them deepen and strengthen their spirituality, so that they may be led towards the very crown of the spiritual life: devotion to the Blessed Trinity.

Our aim is to lead others to holiness, which includes those states of prayer which are both pleasing and profitable to the Church. But, in order to do this, it is necessary not only to touch their hearts, but also to enlighten their intellects. When this does occur for those who desire to make spiritual progress, it often inspires them towards a greater renunciation. For, when Truth touches us, our souls are illuminated and set on fire with love.

In thinking that these supreme dogmas of our Faith should be reserved for an intellectual elite, preachers make a great mistake. If they do act in this way, they are unwittingly drying up the streams of sanctity. For Truth is the source of all love and all devotion. They forget that a special "instinct for God," the germ of the gifts of wisdom and understanding, is implanted in every soul at Baptism. This makes simple souls, sometimes even little children, capable of grasping and enjoying spiritually these great truths. Surely, it is good to make God known as He has revealed and manifested Himself to us.

We hope that these pages may further the desire of St. Paul, the great Apostle, to form Christians "rooted and grounded in love, (having the) power to comprehend with all the saints what is the breadth and length and height and depth, and to know the love of Christ which surpasses knowledge, that (they) may be filled with all the fulness of God" (Ephesians 3:17-19).

With filial affection, we consecrate this little book to Our Blessed Lady—the divine Mother and Seat of Wisdom. At the same time, we invoke St. Catherine of Siena.

O Mary,
   Temple of the Trinity
   and Hearth of the Divine Fire;
Mary,
   Mother of Mercy,

who enshrined Jesus, the source of Life;
Mary,
   in whom was written the Word
   Who gave us the doctrine of life,
explain and reveal Him to us.
Show us the power and goodness of the Father,
   the wisdom of the Word,
   and the love of the Holy Spirit.

PRAYER OF ST. CATHERINE OF SIENA
   O Holy Spirit,
      Come into my heart.
      By Your power,
      draw me to Yourself
      and grant me reverent love.
   O Christ,
      keep me from every evil thought.
      Warm and kindle me
      with Your sweetest Love,
      so that every suffering may seem
      light to me.
   My heavenly Father,
      in everything I may do
      and in every trouble I may have,
      help me this day
      for the love of Christ.

                          Amen.

II. MYSTERY OF CHRIST

+1. God Communicates the Divine Life to the Man Christ

+2. Jesus Communicates to us the Divine Life

+3. Dwelling in Jesus

+4. How Do We Become United with God and Dwell with Him?

II. THE MYSTERY OF CHRIST

I am the Way: walk in Me.
I am the Truth: contemplate Me.
I am the Life: live by Me.

1. God Communicates the Divine Life to the Man Christ

God is the ocean of life. This life, which is also light and love, has a burning desire to spread out and be shared.

From all eternity, the Father gives Himself to the Son. And the Father and the Son together give themselves to the Holy Spirit, filling Him with their one divinity.

Through His inexpressible bounty and compassion, God has also resolved from all eternity to bestow His holy and precious life on the rational beings whom He has created. He has chosen to manifest His Word and to give His Spirit, thereby communicating His nature by intellectual light and love. However, before bestowing Himself on His creatures, the infinite life gave itself in all its fulness to Him who was the "first-born of all creation" (Colossians 1:15). For, because of its union with the Word as a Person, the humanness of Christ participated in the infinite as far as was possible for a created being. The fulness of the divine life poured itself forth on Him, for God willed that in Him "all . . . fulness was pleased to dwell" (Colossians 1: 19). "We have beheld His Glory . . . full of grace and truth" (John 1:14). Jesus has been placed at the summit of all creation and gathered into the sacred Trinity. Thus, Jesus partakes without limit of that Life which, by flooding His heart and soul, saturated (so-to-speak) His intelligence and affections. In this way, Christ Himself becomes an ocean of life.

2. Jesus Communicates to us the Divine Life

Jesus may be above all things. But, that does not isolate Him. Through His magnificent love, God pre-destined Him to be "the firstborn among many breth-ren" (Romans 8:29), the first of a body of which we are the members. "He is the head of the body, the Church" (Colossians 1:18). Now Christ wants His brethren to share in what He has received. The life which was poured out by the blessed Trinity on Christ the Man reaches forth and spreads itself around. From the head, it extends into the members. This same life which filled Christ to the utmost expands and flows into the body formed by the faithful. Thus, we in our turn share in that intimate life of the Three Divine Persons, as well as in their light and in their love.

More than any other mystery, it was this wonderful diffusion of supernatural life which made St. Paul "praise . . . His glorious grace" (Ephesians 1:6) and drew from him those moving words of gratitude (cf Ephesians, Colossians, Philippians). The great apostle never ceased preaching what he termed the "mystery of Christ . . . the mystery hidden for ages and generations, but now made manifest to His saints . . . (the mystery) which is Christ in you. . . ." (Colossians 1:26, 27).

* Both Jesus and the Church form the whole Christ. Jesus is so intimately united to the faithful that they form one single body, animated by the same life flowing through the head and the members alike. For Jesus pours it forth on us and makes it our own. "I am the Vine, you are the branches" (John 15:5). The stem and the branches are one same being—nourished together, working together, and yielding the same fruits fed by the same sap. In the same way, Jesus and the faithful are united in one body. Jesus enjoyed the fulness of this divine life. The light which illuminates and the love which enflames were the supreme delight of His humanity. In us His members, He makes His life flow in such a way that there is the same life in Jesus and in us, in His soul and in our souls, in His heart and in our hearts. There is the same grace and the same communication of love to the Father in union with the Holy Spirit.

3. Dwelling in Jesus

Stay closely united with Christ. These words sum up not only the whole Christian life, but also the whole of Sanctity.

"Abide in Me, and I in you. As the branch cannot bear fruit by itself, unless it abides in the vine, neither can you, unless you abide in Me. . . . He who abides in me, and I in him, he it is that bears much fruit, for apart from me you can do nothing" (John 15:4, 5).

This, then, is the great need: to dwell in Jesus.

To live in Jesus sums up everything and makes everything easier. It places the Christian in habitual communication with God. And it helps him to realize his true vocation, a vocation which could well be expressed in these few words: to enter, through Jesus, into intimate relationship with God our Father in the Holy Spirit, who is everlasting Love.

4. How Do We Become United with God and Dwell with Him?

It is Baptism which first makes us enter into Christ. "Baptism incorporates us with Christ," says St. Thomas. It is from Him that the fulness of life, grace, and virtue flows into us: it is natural that the life of the head should pass into its members. "From His fulness, we have all received. . . . (John 1:15).

The supernatural union given to us at Baptism is strengthened, developed, and perfected by Confirmation. We have all "been made to drink of one Spirit" (1 Corinthians 12:13). Confirmation improves our spiritual growth, making us capable of acting maturely in the spiritual realm. Thus, we can openly and courageously defend the faith which we received at Baptism. "This Sacrament," says St. Thomas, "augments and perfects our spiritual life in all that regards external combats against the enemies of Christ, but it is the work of the Eucharist to perfect man and unite him intimately with God" (Sum. Theol. iii, 79, 1, ad 1).

Therefore, our union with Christ began at Baptism,

was strengthened by Confirmation, and is perfected at the moment of Communion.

It must be noted that Baptism and Confirmation are received once only. And what a shame that is! We can lose the grace with which they have enriched us. This life of grace is continuously exposed to the danger of losing its vitality; it certainly suffers loss from our daily frailties. Since thus it must grow weaker each day, will it not end up by finally disappearing? No. In order to restore it, Our Lord has instituted the most marvellous Sacrament of all: the Sacrament of the Altar, in which all the rest find their consummation and crown.

Its end is twofold: to lead us to perfection and to maintain our union with Christ. Above all, it is the Sacrament of Life. For it is a food that we can receive every day, a *living bread* (John 6:51) instituted explicitly to give us eternal life, *the very life of God Himself*. This living bread does everything for our supernatural life that material bread can do for our bodies: it restores, promotes growth, renews, and gladdens.

To Communion through the Incarnation and Redemption: this is a summary of the whole mystery of Christ. From the sublime heights of the Blessed Trinity, the Incarnate Word descended to man in the Eucharist. Through the Eucharist, man rises upwards to this sacred Trinity, his final end.

From the Trinity to Communion: This was the route which Jesus followed to accomplish His task of sharing His divine life. This was the path created by Divine Love, descending to man whom He wished to save.

From Communion to the Trinity: This is the ascent by which man, purified and strengthened by Christ's companionship, comes to participate in his everlasting reward. This is the way by which human love ascends to God—to God who draws the human heart by the unfailing joy of the beatific vision.

Let us give thanks to the Father, who has qualified us to share in the inheritance of the saints in light. He has delivered us from the dominion of darkness and transferred us to the kingdom of His beloved Son. . . .

He is the image of the invisible God, the first-born of all creation. For in Him all things were created: in heaven and on earth, visible and invisible. . . . All things were created through Him and for Him. He is before all things, and in Him all things hold together.

He is the head of the body, the church. He is the beginning, the first-born from the dead, that in everything he might be pre-eminent. For in Him all the fulness of God was pleased to dwell, and through Him to reconcile all things to himself— whether on earth or in heaven—making peace by the blood of his cross.

And you, who were once estranged and hostile in mind, doing evil deeds, he has now reconciled in his body of flesh by his death, in order to present you holy and blameless and irreproachable before him, provided that you continue in the faith, stable and steadfast, not shifting from hope.

Colossians 1:12, 23

III. THE EUCHARISTIC UNION

+1. Communion is the Primary Means by which Jesus Gives Himself

+2. Communion Gives us the Whole Jesus

+3. Communion Gives us the Three Divine Persons

+4. Communion Associates Us With the Very Life of the Trinity

III. THE EUCHARISTIC UNION

1. Communion is the Primary Means whereby Jesus Gives Himself to Us

Amidst our everyday life, Holy Communion especially unites us with Christ. Eating the *Bread of Life* is the greatest means by which we can enrich ourselves with the divine life.

At that moment, a wonderful union takes place. Even the most intimate unions known to the world cannot be compared to it. If we wish to make an analogy, we might borrow the idea of St. John Chrysostom concerning the union of the two natures in Christ. We could say that we are united to Jesus by Communion —just as He is united to the word by His sacred humanity.

The life of Jesus certainly remains distinct from our life. In the same way, His nature and His soul are also distinct from ours. However, He does establish an incomparable union of love.

To illustrate this *unification of Christ and man* (Council of Florence), the Church Fathers used some wonderful comparisons. "Throw melted wax into melted wax," said St. Cyril of Jerusalem, "and the one interpenetrates the other perfectly. In the same way, when the body and blood of Christ are received, the union is such that Christ is in the recipient and he in Christ. . . . We have the same body and the same blood." St. Cyprian writes, "Our union with Christ unifies affections and wills."

Around the moment we receive Communion, Jesus fills our hearts and our souls so completely that our thoughts and feelings may be said to be His as well. They are, at first, part of Him. And then, He communicates them to us according to the measure of our love. If a person has only a little love, Jesus is forced to accommodate Himself to the narrow limits of his soul and to restrain Himself in the amount He gives. However, it is a different case for the communicant who is detached from both himself and created things and who gives himself unreservedly with a pure heart. To him, in exchange, Jesus gives Himself as only God is able to do. An interchange of life takes place—a communication of gifts and a unity of love which defies human description. The soul permeated by Jesus becomes like fruitful soil germinating both flowers and fruit. It conceives wonderful thoughts and makes ardent acts of love. Can these be said to be ours? Yes, for initially they spring from our own intelligence and affections. Then, insofar as we are united with Christ, they are common to us and to Him. Together we adore, love, and give thanks. Together, we give ourselves to our Father in Heaven. His love and ours, His thoughts and ours, intermingle. Like two grains of incense burned together in the same thurible, they emit one single fragrance towards heaven.

O divine Word,
as Your Father from all eternity is in you
as wholly as you are in Him,
So also, O Jesus, fill me with yourself.
Thus, if you intimately fill all that is mine,
I may be one with you.

M. Olier

2. Communion Gives us the Whole Jesus

At the moment we receive Communion, we really possess *Life itself*. We have within us the incarnate Word, with all He is and with all He does. We have Jesus—both God and man, all the treasures of His divinity, and all the graces of His humanity. In our possession are, in St. Paul's terms, "the unsearchable riches of Christ" (Ephesians 3:8).

Jesus is with us—as man.

The Sacrament of Communion fills us with the heavenly and glorified life of His humanity. It brings into us His heart and His soul. This makes the angels in heaven rejoice. While on earth, some saints also saw the glorified humanity of Jesus in a vision. "It was a beauty human language could not express," said Blessed Angela of Foligno. The remembrance of it caused "an immense joy, a sublime light, an unspeakable and continual delight—a delight compared to which all others are but dross."

This glorified body is animated by a heart which is an abyss of love, by a soul which is indescribably beautiful. It radiates light, life, grace, peace and joy. It is the very sanctuary and paradise of God Himself. Yet, *this* is the body that becomes *our* banquet.

Jesus comes to us—as God.

This is the very crown and culmination of the divine generosity. "Having loved His own who were in the world, He loved them to the end" (John 13:1). That is, He loved them to the utmost limit—the ultimate capacity of love. Thus, we share in the divine life of Jesus, the Word, as the only Son of the Father.

But He Himself said: "I live because of the Father" (John 6:57). From all eternity, the Father gives the Son that life which is His own. He gives it entirely without measure. He gives with a love so generous that, though they remain distinct, they also form one single Divinity. They share the same life, the same fulness of love and joy and peace. Yet, *this* is the life that *we* receive.

O uncreated God!
O God, so lovingly incarnate!
Man has eaten Your flesh and drunk Your blood, that He may be one with You through endless ages.

Blessed Angela of Foligno

3. Communion Gives Us the Three Divine Persons

The Word comes to us. But, He does not come alone. "I am in the Father and the Father in me" (John 14:10). This is such a consoling truth—that wherever Jesus is, so also is His Father. "He who sent me is with me; He has not left me alone.... The Father ... dwells in me ..." (John 8:29; 14:10). However, where the Father and the Son are present, the Holy Spirit is also there too. Thus, the blessed Trinity dwells in the heart of each person receiving Communion. Jesus Himself assures us of this. "If a man loves me, ... my Father will love him, and we will come to him and make our home with him" (John 14:23).

Our soul becomes an indescribably wonderful sanctuary. For, the Three Divine Persons do not dwell in the communicant inactively. The Father continuously gives birth there to the Son, and the Father and Son together breathe forth the Holy Spirit.

The Father expresses a Word for all eternity, a Word which is similar and equal to himself. He manifests

Himself completely through this vital, living Word. It is His own Image, Light, Thought, and Glory. It is the counterpart of Himself—the equivalent splendor of everything perfect in Him, the living mirror of His Being, and the fruit of His affection. Whenever the Father sees this Word, He loves Him with a boundless love. At the same time, the Word returns an infinite love in every way equal to that of His Father. This love is alive, strong, unique, and mutual. It is like an embrace or a kiss lying beyond words—consummating them in the unity of the Holy Spirit. And all this is, of course, a great mystery.

It is the mystery which fills the angels with glory, happiness, and beauty whenever they contemplate it. The angels are marvellous intelligences in that they understand at one glance all the mysteries of created things. Yet, when they fix their gaze on the Three Divine Persons, their desire for this mystery is never satisfied or exhausted. Within the abyss of the Divine Life, their untiring glance always discovers new perfections. These they eagerly contemplate and joyfully praise in song.

It is *this* mystery which is brought to us at Communion.

At all times, "we are the temple of the living God" (2 Corinthians 6:16). For, as St. Thomas says, "by sanctifying grace, the entire Trinity is the guest of our souls." However, if such a thing can be said, this is actually more true at the moment of Communion— because then Jesus comes to us as the *Bread of Life.* He comes in order to explicitly bestow on us that life which He receives from His Father: "He who eats this Bread shall live."

But *how* will he live? "As the living Father sent me,

and I live because of the Father, so he who eats me will live because of me" (John 6:58).

The communicant's soul becomes, so-to-speak, the heaven of the Blessed Trinity. For, the same thing happens in my soul as in heaven: the Father speaks His Word, generates His Son, and thereby gives Him to me. "You are my Son; today I have begotten you. . . . Thou art my beloved Son; with thee I am well pleased" (Psalm 2:7; Luke 3:22). In my soul, the Father and Son now exchange their mutual love as they are held in equal embrace. And their love, radiating like a flame, is the Holy Spirit.

> O eternal God, O almighty Father, O ardent flame of love!
> In the gift you have given, you have manifested your grandeur and bounty.
> As the Infinite and the Eternal Trinity, you have given yourself completely to man.
> To give this gift, you descended into the stable of our humanity, which had become the haunt of mortal sins like animals.
> O eternal Trinity, our supreme love and our true light, enlighten us.
> You who are Wisdom itself,
> grant us wisdom.
> You, who are Omnipotent,
> give us strength.
> Banish our darkness, we beseech You, so that we may know you perfectly, you who are Truth itself.
> And thus, may we always follow you
> in simplicity and sincerity of heart.

St. Catherine of Siena

4. Communion Associates Us With the Very Life of the Trinity

Through this life which is given me, I participate in the marvellous interchange of love of the Three Divine Persons.

Jesus makes me realize His love for His Father. He helps me to penetrate into His heart, showing me His soul burning with love for God. With Him and through Him, I love the Father—who is mine as well as His.

Jesus teaches me to adore, praise, love, and surrender myself. He teaches me to repeat with Him, "Behold, I come to do Thy Will, O my God, ... Into Thy hands I commend my spirit" (Psalm 39:8f; 30:6). Jesus Himself asks His Father to admit me into the mystery of the love of "The Three." "Father, I pray for them also . . . that they may be one in us" (John 17:20, 21).

The Father in His turn includes us in His tender affection for His Son. "No one can come to me," said Jesus, "unless the Father who sent me draws him" (John 6:44). "The Father has loved me" (John 15:9), he adds later—and with what a love! A love which cannot be described, a love which is limitless. Yet, Jesus demands and receives my participation, too, in this unsurpassable tenderness. "Father, may the love with which thou hast loved me be in them . . ." (John 17:26).

Since I am led to the Father by Jesus and to Jesus by the Father, I am immersed, as it were, in the Holy Spirit—the eternal and mutual love of both Father and Son.

It is in the Holy Spirit that you, Father, lead me to Jesus. It is in the Holy Spirit that You, Jesus, guide me to your Father.

The Holy Spirit is your gift. Because He is your union, your consummation, and the seal of your unity, He is also my union, my consummation, and the seal of my unity with You. "He will teach you all things" (John 14:26). He perfects His work by giving me everything. By drawing me, O Jesus, He draws me to the Father. In drawing me while I am with you, O Father, He draws me to Jesus. He attracts me, He possesses me, He makes me one with You. It is through the Holy Spirit that the supreme prayer of Jesus, the great high-priest, is realized:

Father, I pray
  for all those who believe in Me:
that they may all be one;
  even as thou, Father, art in me, and I in Thee,
  that they may be also in us. . . .
The glory which thou hast given me,
  I have given to them,
  that they may be one—even as we are one,
I in them and thou in me,
  that they may become perfectly one,

so that the world may know
that Thou hast sent Me,
and hast loved them
even as Thou hast loved me. . . .

John 17:21-23

O Trinity! Eternal Trinity! O, Fire, abyss of Love!
Would it not have been enough to create us
after your own image and likeness,
making us re-born through grace
by the blood of Your Son?
Was it still necessary that You should give
even the Holy Trinity as food for our souls?
Yet, your love willed this, O Eternal Trinity.
You gave us not only Your Word through the
Redemption and in the Eucharist.
But You also gave us Yourself
in your fulness of love for Your creature.
Truly the soul possesses You
Who are the supreme Goodness.

St. Catherine of Siena

If St. Thomas could write that grace "is the commencement of eternal beatitude," how much more
can this be said of the Eucharistic union. Jesus Himself
said, "He who eats of this bread shall live for ever"
(John 6:52).

The Blessed in heaven and the Church militant on
earth receive the same God and thus partake of the
same life. It is true that the Blessed can actually see
God, while we possess Him only by faith. However,
just like the actual sight of God, Communion gives
Him to us immediately and completely. We receive

Him without any obstacles—other than those of our own frailties and half-heartedness. If our faith were strong enough to cast out this indifference, and if it were ardent enough, the results would be similar to that which takes place in purgatory. For, by our faith, we would prepare the same reception for the Host by which the purifying process of purgatory prepares us for eternal life. Once Communion has filled us with the Eucharistic life, even we on earth would be transformed in God—just like the elect in heaven.

Does it not almost seem as if God had been seized by some divine impatience—and thus could not wait for the hour which should give us the beatific vision? Love has hastened to contract that union which should last eternally. He has made Himself Bread, and He has made Himself Wine. And He says to us, "I am the food of great souls: grow and eat, for you will not change Me into yourself as does bodily food, but you will be changed into Me" (St. Augustine's Confessions). . . . . "Eat, O friends, and drink; drink deeply, O lovers!" (Song of Solomon 5:1).

O Jesus Christ,
  true God and true man, true flesh and blood.
O ineffable union, meeting of immensities.
O my Lord,
  I go from Your humanity to Your divinity,
  from Your divinity to Your humanity.
  I go . . . and I return.
Through contemplation, the soul meets the indescribable divinity which carries within itself all treasures and knowledge.
O imperishable treasure! O divinity!
  You are the source from whom I draw these

nourishing delights, the source
of all I am able to express
and all I am not able to express.
I see the most precious soul of Jesus endowed with
all virtues, all the gifts of the Holy Spirit,
a sacrifice which is holy and without stain.
I see that Body as the price of our redemption.
I see the Blood, from which I draw life and
salvation. And I also see much
that I cannot express.
Truly, here under these veils, is He whom
all the angels adore and before Whom
they tremble.

If only our eyes could be as open as theirs,
what wonders could be worked in us when
this Mystery approaches!
What adoration, what humility. . . .

Blessed Angela of Foligno

IV. THE PERMANENCE OF THE EUCHARISTIC UNION

+A. UNION WITH THE SACRED HUMANITY OF JESUS

+1. Our Union with the Sacred Humanity in virtue of His merits and love.

+2. Our Union with the Sacred Humanity in virtue of His vital action.

+3. Our Union with the Sacred Humanity in the Eucharist

+4. The Intimacy of this Union

+B. UNION WITH THE MOST HOLY TRINITY

+1. The Abiding Presence of the Blessed Trinity

+2. The Divine Circumincession in our Souls

IV. THE PERMANENCE OF THE EUCHARISTIC UNION

The Permanence of the Eucharistic Union

Does the Eucharistic Union last?

Communion is an act—and all acts are passing.

As soon as we have eaten the sacred bread and wine, are we then deprived of the presence of Our Lord? Does this ineffable union last for only a few short moments?

Yet, the Church teaches us to desire the permanence of this union. For, at the moment of Communion, we are bidden to pray:

O Lord Jesus Christ,
    Son of the living God,
by the will of the Father and the work
    of the Holy Spirit your death brought life to the
    world.
By your holy body and blood, free me
    from all my sins and from every evil.
Keep me faithful to your teaching,
    and never let me be parted from you.

"Never let me be parted from you. . . ." Surely, that is the prayer of every loving soul, for love always desires lasting union. Everything that passes has something unfulfilling about it. The person who has received Holy Communion fervently and entered into the intimacy of the Eucharistic mystery feels enkindled with an ardent longing—an insatiable hunger for the sacred Host. Even though daily Communion brings great joys each morning, yet these do not really satisfy that longing. There is a perpetual thirst for Communion, for continuous union with the Eucharistic Mystery.

> Celestial sweetness unalloyed
> Who eat Thee hunger still.
> Who drink of Thee still feel a void
> Which only Thou canst fill.
>
> Lauds Hymn—Feast of the Holy Name of Jesus

Is it too much, then, to think of a continual union with Jesus, a lasting possession of His sacred humanity?

No, not at all. For, the Master Himself both gives and encourages such desires. "He who eats my flesh and drinks my blood abides in me and I in him" (John 6:57).

> O God, thou art my God, I seek thee;
> my soul thirsts for thee;
> my flesh faints for thee,
> as in a dry and weary land where no water is.
> So I have looked upon thee in the sanctuary,
> beholding thy power and glory.
> Because thy steadfast love is better than life,
> my lips will praise thee.
>
> Psalm 63

O God of love,
my Savior, my joy, my delight for all eternity.
You alone can quench my thirst and fill my soul.
Yet, the more I feed on You, the more I hunger;
the more I drink at your spring, the more I thirst.
Come, then, Lord Jesus—
Come.

St. Gertrude

The permanence of the eucharistic union is both possible and real. Even when the sacred species are consumed, the communicant may remain closely united to the sacred humanity of Jesus.

However, we must understand this union perfectly.

The sacred humanity is present in heaven; it is also present in the tabernacles on our altars. In heaven it has a glorious form; in the tabernacles it has a eucharistic form. Such is the teaching of theology. Once the Bread and Wine are actually consumed, of course, Christ's humanness ceases to be with the communicant in its eucharistic state. Undoubtedly, it would be theologically incorrect to suppose that the sacred humanity remains in our hearts just as it remains in the consecrated host.

However, we can say correctly that we dwell in permanent union with the humanity of Our Lord. For, even if He does not stay in us in His bodily substance, yet He continuously abides in us through the outpouring of His love and by the workings of His power. He always dwells in us through the lights and graces He sends us unceasingly from the tabernacle.

The eternal Father said to St. Catherine of Siena:

Consider what excellencies the soul receives in this Bread of Life, this nourishment of angels. In receiving this sacrament, it dwells in Me and I in it. As the fish is in the sea and the sea in the fish, so am I in the soul and the soul in Me—the ocean of peace. After Communion, grace remains. For, having received this Bread of Life in the state of grace, the soul retains grace when the appearance of bread is consumed.

I leave the imprint of my grace, as the soft wax retains the imprint when the seal is withdrawn. In the same way, through this sacrament, in the soul remain behind the ardour of My divine charity, the loving mercy of the Holy Spirit, the intellectual light of created Wisdom—that is, My only Son.

A. UNION WITH THE SACRED HUMANITY OF JESUS

1. Our Union with the Sacred Humanity in Virtue of His Merits and Love

The sacred humanity is always present to us, through the incessant action of His merits and the perpetual radiation of His love. Christ, says St. Paul, "always lives to make intercession for (us)" (Hebrews 7:25). In heaven, in the Blessed Sacrament, He does not cease pleading for us by recalling His merits to His Father, Who is then almost compelled to help us. He shows us that human nature which He once took upon Himself—the humanness which merited for us the signs of His sacrifice as well as the sacred wounds. He manifests the ardent desire in His Soul for our salvation, a desire which is far more than a prayer. For, it is an appeal to His infinite merits which is granted immediately.

He intercedes on behalf of all whom He has redeemed. For all, as for each individually, He has a special regard and a special outpouring of His love. "I am the good shepherd. . . . The good shepherd calls his own sheep by name and leads them out. . . . I know My sheep. . . ." (John 10:3, 14). This is not simply knowledge, St. Thomas says, but a loving recognition in which the heart takes part as much as the intellect. Ceaselessly, Jesus watches me from the depths of the tabernacle with a look that penetrates to my inmost being, a glance both attentive and tenderly affectionate. "Lift up the light of thy countenance upon us, O Lord!" (Psalm 4:7). Not a single thought or act escapes Jesus. There is not one of my desires which He does not know better than I do myself. He takes count of all my varying feelings, my needs, my dangers, and my aspirations. He does this not simply to observe them, but to give me the graces I need for all these changing states. And this He does through the instrumentality of His glorified humanity.

At every moment He loves me. And with what a love! Certainly, the uncreated love of the Word is always with us. It is an ineffable blessing to know that it is beyond our power to escape from it. But, as man also, Jesus loves me. He pours forth floods of tenderness from His tabernacle; He envelops me with love. This love never decreases; there is never a moment in which I can say that Jesus is not thinking of me right now. Even when I am asleep at night, He watches. "The journey on which you go is under the eye of the Lord" (Judges 18:6). And He looks upon us thus with a love which never grows weary. *I* often forget and offend, but *He* continues to bestow His graces. His love helps me all the time. It has the tenderness of brother, friend, and spouse. Night and day I am under its influence. How precious is this union between the soul and God, flowing unceasingly from the love of the Sacred Heart!

The Lord is my Shepherd,
    I shall not want.
He makes me lie down in green pastures.
He leads me beside still waters;
    he restores my soul. . . .
Even though I walk through the valley
    of deep darkness, I will fear no evil.
For thou art with me: thy rod and thy staff,
    they comfort me.

                                        Psalm 23

2. Our Union with the Sacred Humanity in Virtue of His Vital Action

There is a still more intimate way in which the sacred humanity of Jesus can be present: the mysterious presence of His vital action.

"I am the Life" (John 14:6), said Jesus. And during His ministry on earth, His humanness repeatedly showed forth its supernatural power. His touch was enough to perform the greatest miracles.

"Power came forth from Him and healed . . . all" (Luke 6:19). Today, far from being lessened, this power knows no obstacle and no cessation. It is continually giving life and energy to everything everywhere. Fortunately, none of us can escape from that action or "the contact of His power" (as some theologians call it).

Christ's vital action is the center of the supernatural universe. It is the sun which illuminates all the supernatural creatures of God. It is the supernatural atmosphere—without which there would be no life, no light, no security, and no relation with God.

Christ's humanness, placed at the summit of creation in immediate contact with the divinity and flowing with divine life, became itself the source of life. It became the point of departure for the divine gifts. Life springs, as it were, in great floods from the soul and heart of Jesus. It is a deluge of light and love, descending like a cataract in varying degrees on all the elect. It fills the children of God in all parts of the earth with light and joy.

Like the sun casting forth its rays or some overflowing spring, the heart of Jesus unceasingly pours forth a great bounty of grace. This first rejoices the elect in heaven, and then spreads itself around on earth through the seven rivers of the sacraments and a thousand other streams—all flowing from the ocean of His Love. In this way, the predestined are sanctified, and the virtues of the Christian life are perfected.

Whereas on Calvary the sacred humanity merited life for us, now it dispenses life. "Grace was given to each of us according to the measure of Christ's gift" (Ephesians 4:7). What are the sacraments—if not the Humanness of Christ employed to sanctify mankind?

Even outside the sacraments, this life is always active. Through interior illuminations and efficacious movements, this life never ceases to influence souls. If I am now in a state of grace, the sacred humanity is the cause. We receive no supernatural influence which does not come from His heart, no ray of divine light which does not come from His soul. Without Christ's humanness I am powerless—even to say "Lord Jesus." It is the source of all spiritual activity for me, all progress, all growth in the things of God. From beginning to end, my life wells up from this spring. If Jesus' sacred humanity were to withdraw for one moment, or to deprive me of His light, I would fall again into death.

"As the head commands the members," said the Council of Trent, "as the vine penetrates all its branches with its sap, so every moment Jesus Christ exercises His influence on all the just. He prepares, assists, and crowns all good works, making them agreeable and meritorious before God" (Sess. vi. Can. 16).

"*Christus vita vestra:* Christ is your life," said the Apostle. As St. Thomas adds, this is "because He is the author and conserver of your life: *quia epse est actor vitae vestrae*" (St. Thomas, Comm. In Coloss. iii. 4).

> O eternal Trinity, all-powerful God,
> > we are dead trees, while You are
> > the Tree of Life.
> O infinite God, how amazing to see in Your light
> > the tree of your creature.
> O supreme Purity, for the branches of that tree,
> > You gave the powers of the soul,
> > intelligence, memory, and will.
> And what fruits should these branches bear?
> > The memory should retain You, the intelligence know You, the will Love You.
> When first planted by the gardener,
> > the condition of this tree was most happy.
> But also, O my God, it is diseased.
> > It now bears a poisonous fruit,
> > so that a tree of life has become a tree of death.
> But, Eternal Trinity, You love Your creature
> > even to folly.
> Impelled by the same love which created it,
> > You saved the dying tree by grafting upon it
> > Your divinity.

You saved it—even when evil fruits were produced because it had separated itself from You
as the Giver of Life.
Life-giving graft,
You mingled sweet sap with our bitterness,
splendour with darkness,
wisdom with folly,
life with death,
and the infinite with the finite.
After the injury which Your creature had done,
what made You give Life by this union?
Love!
Love alone was the marvellous graft
that vanquished death.
But that did not satisfy the flame of Your charity,
O eternal Word.
For, you then watered the tree
with Your own Blood,
and the warmth of that Blood made it fruitful
so long as man was united and lived in You.
His heart and affections must be bound to You
by the cords of obedience and charity.
They must be united to the celestial graft,
so that the branches bear fruit.
O infinite Love,
what marvels You have worked
in Your creatures!
Why will not men water their tree
at the fountain of Blood?
Eternal Life is poured out for us poor creatures.
Yet . . . we ignore it
and refuse to benefit from it.
I have sinned.

O, My Lord, have pity upon me.
Jesus love!
O love of Jesus. . . .

St. Catherine of Siena

3. Our Union with the Sacred Humanity in the Eucharist

Where is this sacred humanity, the source of my supernatural life? Doubtless, it is in Heaven. However, in the Blessed Sacrament, Jesus is closer and more accessible to me. He is there living and working. He is there precisely that He may be in close contact with me. He is there to nourish my spiritual life and to make me participate in the life of His heart and soul. "I am the bread of life . . . the living bread which came down from Heaven. He who eats of this bread shall live forever" (John 6:48, 51, 55).

Above all, it is at the moment of Communion that this life overflows into me. However, after the sacred species are consumed, He still dwells in my soul, for the sacred humanity continues to make me share in His life by means of His grace. I rest in communication with Him as the branch communes with the sap of the vine. Is not the union between the sap and the branch a lasting one? Is not the union between the head and the members a real and permanent union? The union of the communicant with the humanity of Jesus is just as real, permanent, and efficacious. Between the soul of the Communicant and the soul of Christ, there is an incessant communication—a flowing and re-flowing of life. As long as the life is the same, external distance does not really matter. Yet, it is essentially the same life, for it is the same grace which is in the Host and in my soul.

Lord, Almighty God,
    Life is not for our destruction—but
    for our living.
You remain ever one and the same in Yourself,
    but there goes forth from You continually
    a power and virtue, which by its contact
    is our strength and good. . . .
The living God is lifegiving.
You are the fount and centre,
    as well as the seat of all good.
And so, make me like Yourself, O, My God,
    since, in spite of myself,
    such You can make me, such I can be made. . . .
Lord, I am asking for Yourself,
    for nothing short of You, O My God,
    who has given Yourself wholly to us.
Enter into my heart substantially and personally
    and fill it with fervour by filling it with You.
You alone can fill the soul of men,
    and You have promised to do so.
You are the living Flame,
    and You are ever burning with love of man.

        Enter into me and set me on fire
        after Your pattern and likeness.

                Cardinal Newman

4. The Intimacy of this Union

Nothing that is human and terrestial can be compared to the closeness of this union, for the sacred humanity acts directly upon the soul. Though they have received marvellous gifts, the angels themselves are unable to act immediately on my mind and move it spontaneously to think and believe. Still less have they power to act from within upon my will. It is God alone who can control and move the centres of energy in the soul.

However, the sacred humanity has received a communication of this divine power. In this way, it not only reaches over me the protection of prayer and an infinite tenderness. It also exercises its divine efficacy in penetrating the depths of my soul and will.

The union of husband and wife, or the union of soul and body, are not as intimate as the union of my soul with the sacred humanity. This is because grace, the fruit of His sacrifice now communicated to me, penetrates the very center of my soul. Just as perfume pervades the vessel that contains it, as the ray pierces through the crystal giving it purity and brilliance, and as the fire penetrates iron warming and enkindling it, so too grace from the Eucharist flows into my soul. It possesses, penetrates, and fills; in the words of St. Thomas, it "transforms and inebriates with God" (St. Thomas in Joann. cap. VI, Lect. 7).

This grace is my true life—much more so than the life of my body or even the natural life of my soul. It is the me of myself, the souls of my soul, as Contenson said. In this way, in its depths and in its most intimate centre, my life is the grace which flows to it each moment from the Host. Jesus said to Blessed Angela of Foligno: "I am closer to your soul than your soul is to itself." Or, as St. Paul exclaimed, "For me to live is Christ!" (Phil. 1:21). With equal truth and the same interior joy, we too can say, "Life for me is the Eucharist." For, I am merely repeating the words of the Master Himself, "He who eats Me shall live because of Me" (John 6:58).

> O Lord Jesus, O immense sea,
>> why do You delay receiving this drop of water
>> into Your plenitude?
> The sole desire of my soul, a desire as ardent
>> as it is sweet, is to escape from myself and enter
>> into You.
> Open for me a place of refuge:
>> Your beloved Heart.
>> Mine exits no longer.
> It is Yours, Yours my beloved—
>> who captured it once and still holds it.
> From You it derives its life.
>> Worthless as it is,
>> You have transformed it

into Your divine essence.
My soul in its activities
  lives only for You.

How indescribable is this union!
  This intimate familiarity with You is superior
  to any other mode of life. . . .
What joy it is to breathe the divine peace and
  loving tenderness which are in You.

O, if I could only obtain here below
  what I desire:
  to dwell
    by an indissoluble union
      united to You.

St. Gertrude

B. UNION WITH THE MOST HOLY TRINITY

It might be helpful to note that, usually, it is not at the time of Communion that the Holy Trinity begins to live in us. Rather, this supernatural presence is produced the moment the soul enters a state of grace. In speaking of the Eucharistic union with reference to the Blessed Trinity, we simply wish to say that Communion is the most effective means of bringing about that sublime work of making the soul supernatural. Each time we approach the holy table, it augments the presence of the Three Divine Persons. There is thus a fresh influx of the Divine Life—which, in theological language, would be called a new "invisible mission."

1. The Abiding Presence of the Blessed Trinity

Unlike the physical presence of Christ's humanity, the presence of the Three Divine Persons is not limited to the intact Eucharistic species. They lived in our soul before Communion, and they remain after the Host has disappeared. However, they are present more intimately, for Communion has increased their influence and efficacy. After Communion, the soul's capacity to receive God is expanded. Our Lord said that He, the Father, and the Holy Spirit would come to anyone who loves them. "And we will make our home with him" (John 14:23).

The Three do more than visit us. They actually make their home with us. Our soul becomes a heaven; our life becomes a beginning and prelude of the eternal happiness. Our Lord said, "The Kingdom of Heaven is within you" (Luke 17:21). This is why St. Paul could write, "God's temple is holy, and that temple you are. Your body is a temple of the Holy Spirit within you." (1 Corinthians 3:17; 6:19).

In this temple, the three Divine Persons do not remain inactive. They act unceasingly, each according to His own character. The mystery of the Trinity is realized in the activity and love which the Three Persons bring to the soul. The soul is loved differently by each of them—yet, with a single love. This love is single because, each time the Three Persons act exteriorly to themselves, they act as one. At the same time, it is a triple outpouring of love which reveals something of the characteristics proper to each of the Three Persons.

The Father comes as the source of life and peace. The Creator, after making the creature, establishes it in its appropriate surroundings. The Father encircles His child with goodness and inexpressible tenderness.

The Word is a source of light. The Father's thought, His living Word, His image, He unites Himself with my mind—thus giving me a supernatural knowledge of the divinity.

The Holy Spirit is the source of love. He is the love of the Father and the Son, their mutual embrace, the eternal expression of their love, and the consummation of their life. He unites Himself to my will, in order to introduce me to the supernatural love of the Father and Son.

> O Eternal Trinity, One God,
>> One in essence and three in Person,
>> You are like a vine with three branches.
>
> You made man to Your own image and likeness.
>> By the three powers of his soul,
>> he resembles both Your Trinity and Unity.
>
> By his memory, he resembles and unites himself

to the Father, to whom power is attributed.
By intelligence, he resembles and unites himself
to the Son, who is wisdom.
By his will, he resembles and is united with the
Holy Spirit, to whom mercy is assigned,
and who is the love of the Father and the Son....
O eternal God,
You are the tranquil ocean,
where souls live and are nourished,
finding in You repose in union and love.

St. Catherine of Siena

2. The Divine Circumincession in our Souls*

At Communion, a wonderful resemblance to the circumincession of the Three Persons in the Trinity takes place.

In God, there is no immobility. Rather, there is an eternal movement, an everlasting circulation of love. For, it is the nature of love to go forth and share itself. If He stayed only within Himself, the Father would not be God, He gives Himself lovingly to His Son, whom He never ceases to engender. Similarly, the Son would not be God if He did not have a similar relation to the Father. Between them, there is an irresistible and mutual attraction, a force of love which unites and consummates them in unity. This unity of their mutual love, the substance of the divine life, is the Holy Spirit.

---

*Circumincession is a theological term indicating that the Three Persons of the Trinity mutually dwell in one another in such a way that there is a kind of reciprocal interflow among them. At Communion, something similar takes place between God and the soul.

However, this love which comes from the breathing forth of their mutual and infinite love, has a special function. As the Holy Spirit uniting the Father and Son in inexpressible joy, this love communicates to the soul a movement similar to the mutual attraction of Father and Son. Thus, the soul is allowed to participate in these mutual and intimate relations. In heaven, this mutual communication is perfect. Without any veil and without any obstacle at all, the blessed contemplate the Three Divine Persons. With the Father, they admire, love, and rejoice in the great splendour of the Word. With the Word, they admire, love, and rejoice in the perfection of the Father. The Father draws them towards the Son, the Son towards the Father. This eternal movement of love unites them in the Father and Son, consummating them in the unity of the Holy Spirit.

On earth, we have merely the beginning of this wonderful joy. Yet, we also have a true participation. For the life of grace here below and that of glory in heaven are one and the same; grace begins what glory achieves. Thus, there is already in us something of this wonderful mystery of the circumincession of the Three Persons. Jesus Himself helps us to realize this, "No one comes to the Father except through Me" ... "No one can come to Me unless my Father draws him" (John 14:6; 6:44). In other words: You will never go to My Father unless you enter into the movement of love which unites Me to Him. And you will never come to Me unless the Father draws you into the love with which He turns to Me, and which is consummated in the unity of the Holy Spirit. Thus, the soul which loves the Three Divine Persons is drawn by the Holy Spirit into that intercommunicating movement of vision and love which constitutes the happiness of God, a happiness which is communicated to the angels and the Blessed.

Consequently, we can say with St. Augustine, "The saints bear God within them. Their soul is a heaven, for God inhabits it." Or, as St. John says, "We have fellowship with the Father and with His Son Jesus Christ" (1 John 1:3). Between the Three and ourselves, there is a society, a familiar intercourse, a common life.

Holy Father,
  receive me into Your tender paternity.
  Thus, once I have finished the race
    which I have begun to run for love of You,
    may I receive You, my reward,
    as an eternal heritage.

Most loving Jesus,
  take me into Your loving fraternity.
  Bear with me the trials and heat of the day.
  Be my consolation in all my troubles,
    my companion and guide
    during the pilgrimage of this life.

Holy Spirit, Love of God,
  take me into Your loving Charity.
  Be the master, teacher, and tender friend
    of my soul
      always. . . .

                                                St. Gertrude

V. TO MAINTAIN AND PERFECT UNION

+A. TO MAINTAIN UNION

+1. Our Model Jesus Christ

+2. Recollection: A Condition for the Life of Union

+3. Union During Work

+4. Union in Temptation

+5. Union in Bodily Suffering

+6. Union in Grief of Heart

+7. Union in Desolation of Soul

+8. Union in Joy

+B. TO PERFECT UNION

+1. Repetition of Acts of Desire

+2. Repetition of Acts of Love

+3. The Invisible Divine Missions

V. TO MAINTAIN AND PERFECT UNION

To Maintain and Perfect Union

In order for our souls to remain united with Christ's humanity and the Blessed Trinity, it is sufficient to remain in a state of grace. Only mortal sin destroys this permanent union. Whether we think of it or not, we are incorporated into Christ and live in Him. However, the fruits which we gather differ very considerably. They are in proportion to the consciousness or unconsciousness of this union. That is, they depend upon whether or not we realize this Presence of God within us. We may be united to God as the child is one with the mother as he sleeps in her arms. Or, we may be united with God as was the beloved Apostle: at the Last Supper, he reclined his head on the breast of the Master and listened to the secrets of His Heart.

Without doubt, that first unconscious union is very precious. But, how much more perfect is the second! This alone can lead to perfection, to sanctity. We can draw fully from the infinite resources of Communion and the union it establishes only by the constant exercise of our free will. Or, to use the language of theologians, we must make this union more and more actual. We must not content ourselves with a state-of-grace only. Our love must be awake and actuated by the desire to live unceasingly with the Blessed Trinity through Jesus.

Now this would be relatively easy if we could spend our lives before the tabernacle, without constant external interruptions from external work and occupations. But, for the majority of us, this is far from the case. After Communion, we must return to our brethren and often to very absorbing duties. Providence has assigned a definite work to each of us, and it is not our place to turn from it. Christ comes to help us accomplish it, and He wants us to do our best.

But now a difficulty arises. Should we cease contemplating the wonderful mysteries which Communion has brought into our souls? Must we leave God to serve our neighbour? Yes, indeed we must. However, we must still try to dwell with God, uniting external work with interior contemplation. To put it briefly: we must lead an active exterior life without diminishing the interior. But how is this to be done? Let us try and explain how we should direct our efforts:

    A. How to maintain union with God in the midst of our occupations and in the changing phases of life;

    B. How to perfect this union.

Teach me, O Lord, the way of thy statutes,
    and I will keep it to the end.
Give me understanding, that I may keep thy law

and observe it with my whole heart.
Incline my heart to thy testimonies. . . .
Give me life in Thy way. . . .
Behold, I long for thy precepts;
  in thy righteousness, give me life!

Psalm 119

"The knowledge of God! This, O Lord, is the joy of joys. Knowledge precedes, love follows—love the transformer. He who truly knows is ardent in love."

Blessed Angela of Foligno

A. TO MAINTAIN UNION

1. Our Model Jesus Christ

Here, as in all things, Jesus is our model. He dwells always with His Father. "I am in the Father and the Father in Me" (John 14:10). The union of His Soul with the Word, and consequently with the Father "and with the Holy Spirit," was always perfect. Lying on the straw of the manger at Bethlehem, bending over the carpenter's bench at Nazareth, walking along the paths of Judea, or hanging on the Cross, He could always say, "I am in the Father."

God was continuously in His thoughts. No work or suffering could for even an instant turn Him away from God. His Soul never ceased contemplating the splendors of the Beatific Vision. He saw everything on earth in the divine light, estimating and judging according to the eternal thought of His Father. "As I hear, I judge. . . . What I say, therefore, I say as the Father has bidden Me" (John 5:30; 12:50).

Christ's will was always so intimately united to His Father's that he loved or accomplished only what the Father loved or desired. "He who has sent me is with me; He has not left me alone. For, I always do the things that are pleasing to Him" (John 8:29).

This is the Man whom the Jews saw working as a carpenter, traversing the roads like any other, suffering fatigue, hunger, thirst, and pain. And yet, He was always unchangeably peaceful and unspeakably happy.

Such is the model for every Christian.

O Jesus, living in Mary,
  come and live in us
  through your holiness, the fulness
  of your powers, the reality of your virtues,
  the perfection of your ways.
Overcome all the power of the enemy
  by your Spirit
    to the glory of the Father.

M. Olier

2. Recollection: A Condition for the Life of Union

To live constantly with God and in God is the ideal set before the communicant. In order to attain this, the practice of recollection is a primary necessity.

The soul is "recollected" when it gathers together all its faculties and enters *into itself to find God there*. The avoidance of useless conversations, the withdrawal from worldly amusements, and the practice of silence are the elementary duties of everyone seeking to live a truly Christian life.

To imagine that a pious and a worldly life can co-exist is a dangerous illusion. It is necessary to choose between God and the world.

"I will lead her into solitude, and there I will speak to her heart" (cf Hosea 2:14).

However, an external silence is not enough. What use is it if inner voices make an uproar? It is necessary to establish silence within. This means that we must banish preoccupations, useless thoughts, day-dreams, and all the vain work of the imagination—which often troubles us more than prolonged external conversations. To give free reign to one's imagination, amuse oneself with remembrances of the past, indulge useless thoughts, follow up some purely natural desire, build castles in Spain, worry about the future—all this draws a veil between the soul and God. It is an obstacle to perfect union.

Unfortunately, there are persons who, while fulfilling their religious duties and usually possessing the state of grace, yet lead a mediocre life. They draw little fruit from their habitual union with God. And perhaps they end up by losing their piety from lack of recollection and silence. God *is* in them, but they do not know how to dwell in Him. The psalmist said, "My soul is continually in my hands; and I have not forgotten Thy law" (Psalm 119:109). This is a verse which throws light on our fundamental obligation to keep ourselves consciously in the presence of the Blessed Trinity.

The sincere Christian ought to keep a ceaseless watch over himself, so that he may constantly and continuously govern his interior faculties. The useless play of the imagination enfeebles the soul. When this is weakened, and thus drawn in different directions, it is incapable of giving itself up as it should to the work of loving God. Through recollection, the scattered forces which had been uselessly wasted and dispersed are re-united and led to God. Now that it has been re-established in possession of itself and its unity, the soul can then hold intimate communion with its guests: the Three Divine Persons, who never cease urging it to converse with them.

Hear, O daughter, consider,

and incline your ear;
forget your people and your father's house,
   and the king will desire your beauty.
Since he is your Lord,
   bow to him . . .

Psalm 45:10

"Do you wish to listen to God? Keep silence, banish creatures, and turn towards Him. The Father uttered one word: His Word, His Son. He utters it eternally, in an eternal silence. It is in this silence that the soul hears." (Maxims of St. John of the Cross)

"The law of prayer," said Blessed Angela of Foligno, "is one of unity. God requires the entire man, not a part of him. The whole heart must go forth in prayer. If that does not happen, nothing is obtained. Realize that God alone is your supreme need. To find Him, and to unite all the faculties in Him, is the one thing necessary.

To attain recollection, it is essential to cut away all extravagances, all curiosity, all unnecessary acts and occupations. In short, man must put away all that can divide him."

Everyone should follow the advice of St. Catherine of Siena: she loved to recommend to her disciples the building of *an interior cell*, where they should live with God alone and be occupied with the "one thing necessary" (Luke 10:42). There, each person could hold his soul within his hands and could say with the Spouse in the Canticle, seeking the Beloved, "I knew not" (Cant. 6:11). That is, I have forgotten everything except God and the things of God. Or, as St. Paul says, "I count everything as loss . . . that I may gain Christ" (Philippians 3:8).

"If anyone wishes to arrive at the state of union, it is absolutely necessary that he disengage himself from all things and that he recollect himself interiorly. Within himself, he must hold before the eyes of his soul nothing but Jesus covered with wounds. Then, applying himself with all his energy to go by Him, with Him, and in Him as Man to the Godhead, he passes by the wounds of His humanity to the inmost sanctuary of the Divinity" (Concerning Union with God, Ch. 11).

O my God, Trinity,
   whom I adore,
help me to entirely forget myself,
   so that peaceably and unchangeably
   I may establish myself in You,
      as though my soul were already in eternity.
Grant that nothing may trouble my peace
   or make me part from You, my Immutable One.
Rather, each moment, may I plunge myself
   further into Your mysteries.
   Tranquillize my soul.
Make it Your heaven, Your abode, the place
   of Your repose.
   May I never leave You there alone,
      but be there with all my faculties,
      given up in adoring Faith
      to Your creative action.

O Christ, my loved One, crucified by love,
   I would wish to be that spouse of Your Heart.
I desire to glorify You, to die with love for You.
But, feeling my own powerlessness, I ask You
   to clothe me with Yourself,
   to identify the movements

of my soul with Yours.
Penetrate me, so that my life
   may be a ray of Your life.
Come into me as Adorer, Redeemer, and Savior.

O Eternal Word, Word of God,
   I would pass my life in listening to You.
I desire to be such that I may learn all from You.
O beloved Star of my soul,
   Let me never be separated from Your light.
Grant that, by the illumination of Your rays,
   I may travel through the nights
   and the desolate spaces of life.

O consuming Fire, Spirit of Love,
   come down upon me.
   Make my soul, as it were, an incarnation
   of Your Word.
Supernaturalize me,
   so that I may renew this mystery.

And You, O Father,
   bend down to Your weak and small creature.
See only in her Your dearly-beloved
   in whom You are "well-pleased."

O my Three, my happiness, my all!
   Infinite solitude,
   Immensity where I lose myself.
I give myself up to You.
Bury Yourself in me, that I may be buried in You,
   until in Your light I shall contemplate the abyss
                              of your grandeurs.
                        —Sister Elizabeth of the Trinity

3. Union During Work

a. *Our Exemplar*

Jesus came upon this earth to work. "I am poor and have laboured from my youth" (Psalm 88:16). He was devoted to His work. Nothing could retain or hinder His accomplishing it, not even the love He had for His Mother. "How is it that you sought me? Did you not know that I must be about my Father's business" (Luke 2:49)? He loved His work. And, in order to perform it as He wished, He needed a holy freedom.

b. *Intention for Work*

Christ's work was an act of adoration of His heavenly Father, a recognition of His sovereign rights. Above all else, Jesus wished to serve God, for such is the real duty of every creature. "I am in the midst of you as a servant. . . . The Son of man came not to be served, but to serve . . ." (Matthew 20:28). In the divine service lay His joy and His delight. Whatever was the particular work, whether cutting wood with His adopted father, or preaching to the crowds, or going on journeys, or carrying His Cross, His word was religiously accomplished in a spirit of love and inexpressible humility. His sole intention was to glorify God.

Thus, at the Last Supper, He was able to testify to the fulfillment of His task. "Father, I glorified thee on earth, having accomplished the work which thou gavest me to do!" (John 17:4). He laboured for His Father because He loved Him. Love was always luring him onwards. Consequently, when He began His great work, the Passion, He could say, "That the world may know that I love the Father. . . . Arise, let us go hence" (John 14:31).

For Him, laborious toil was a work of justice. In the first place, His sacred humanness felt bound to spend itself serving One Who had endowed Him so richly and gratuitously. Secondly, He had come here below as redeemer and universal penitent. Having taken our sins upon Him, His task became one of reparation. Work became His lot—toil which was difficult, troublesome, and painful. Also, He felt an immense joy in spending Himself without limit, labouring without relaxation. Work was His food—and the joy of His heart. "My food is to do the work of Him who sent me and to accomplish His work" (John 4:34).

The Christian should have "the same mind as Christ" (cf. Philippians 2:5), in order to unite his intentions with those of the Divine Workman. Because it is the service of God, let us love work above all else. It should be a duty for us, a work of religion, a sign of humility and dependence. It should be an acknowledgement of the divine rights of the Creator over His creatures.

We should love the fatigue and the trials which we

may face during the course of our work. For it is just and fitting that we should atone for the sins we may have committed. Even though He was merely "clothed," so-to-speak, with our sins, Christ as the Lamb without stain desired to suffer so much for us. Thus, how much more do we, who are truly sinners, need the fatigue of work.

c. How to Work

It is essential to realize that, in His work, Jesus always dwelt with His Father. It would be erroneous to conclude that, once Christ has left Nazareth to begin His apostolic life, He diminished to any extent His prayer life. No, His active life never lessened His contemplative. In the depths of His soul, there always rested the same deep and permanent love for His Father which supported Him in the various phases of His life and was the foundation of all its mysteries. The time He gave to His Father during His private life was more exclusive, but not more abundant. In leaving Nazareth, He assumed more fatiguing labors. But, this did not diminish His interior life. Suppressing as far as possible the difference between the times of prayer and the time of work, we can and should always converse with our interior Guests. "Whatsoever you do in word or in work, do all in the name of the Lord Jesus Christ, giving thanks to God and the Father by Him" (Colossians 3:17).

The kind of work we do matters little. Whether we study, do manual labor, talk, or eat, we need never cease loving God.

Is it a question of doing good to our neighbor? Let us not abandon God in the process, but rather bring God to our neighbour. We must keep in mind the fundamental law at the root of all Christian action: apostolic work which does not have its source in prayer is not only unfruitful, but often harmful. Any "active" life which develops at the expense of the interior life is contrary to God's will. What we give to our neighbour should never diminish what we give to God. Our action should never be separated from our prayer. Rather, action should be prayer which manifestly makes itself exterior, thereby overflowing into the lives of our brethren.

There may be some people who, even with a charitable intention, devote themselves unnecessarily to works incompatible with recollection and thereby lose their interior life. If such is the case, they should hasten to drop all such works, bearing in mind the words of St. Bernard, *"Maledicta occupatio quae te retrahit a deo"* ("Accursed be the occupation which leads us away from God").

In the Church, action is necessary. However, even more needful are prayer and contemplation.

> O Holy Father,
>> by that love through which You have shined
>>> on me the light of Your countenance,
>> help me to continually advance
>>> in all holiness and virtue.
>
> O Christ, O Jesus!
>> By that love which urged You to redeem me
>>> by Your blood,
>> reclothe me with the purity of Your holy life.
>
> O Holy Spirit! Whose power and holiness
> are equal!
>> Through that Love which united me
>>> to You at Baptism,

grant me the power to love You
with all my heart.
to cling to you with all my soul,
to spend all my energy in serving
and loving You,
to live only for Your will.
Thus, when I die, I may be clothed
with a stainless robe
and fully prepared for the divine nuptials.

St. Gertrude

4. Union in Temptation

Is it more difficult to maintain union with God in temptation? No, not if we hold firmly to our faith and realize that, at times, God makes "darkness His covering around him" (Psalm 18:11). He hides Himself in our hearts and allows the devil to approach us. But still, He remains within us.

In the life of St. Catherine of Siena, there is a helpful incident bearing upon this question. St. Catherine was assailed by terrible temptations against purity. At last the storm passed, and Our Lord appeared to her.

"O Lord," she cried, "where were You when my heart was filled with such impure thoughts?"

"I was in your heart."

"Yes, Lord, You are Truth itself, and I bow before You. But how can I believe this—since my heart was filled with such detestable thoughts?"

"But—these thoughts and temptations, did they cause you joy or sorrow, pleasure or pain?"

"Terrible sorrow—terrible pain!"

"Know then, my daughter, that you suffered

because I was hidden in the midst of your heart. If I had been absent, the thoughts that had penetrated there would have given you pleasure. However, it was My presence which made them unbearable to you. I was acting in you, defending your heart against the enemy. Never have I been closer to you."

These divine words show us the course to follow in temptation. We must keep ourselves closely united to Jesus. When the devil attacks our supernatural life, who is it he attacks—if not God Himself? It is Christ in us whom he persecutes and wants to crucify again. What he tries to extinguish in us is the very life of Christ. Thus, the secret of victory is to remain undisturbed. It is neither to directly repulse nor discuss the suggestions of the evil one, but to adhere with all our will to Him who has already overcome. He will do more than we can to save the life He has communicated to us. More than ever, it is the right moment to practice St. Paul's advice, "As therefore you received Christ Jesus the Lord, so live in Him, rooted and built up in Him and established in the faith" (Colossians 2: 6, 7). Whoever dwells calmly united to Christ and trusts in Him will never be vanquished by the demon. "For greater is He that is in you than he that is in the world" (1 John 4:4).

> Though a host encamp against me,
>   my heart shall not fear.
> Though war arise against me,
>   yet I will be confident. . . .
> That the Lord will hide me in His shelter
>   in the day of trouble. . . .

> Psalm 26:3, 5

St. Gertrude wrote:

"I give thanks to Your protection, O adorable and incomprehensible Trinity, for not permitting temptation beyond my powers—although You do allow this for my advance in virtue. When you see that all our hope is based on You, with unparalleled generosity, You take charge of the conflict. And, bearing the brunt Yourself, You bestow on us the prize of victory."

Having requested the grace to remain always united with God, St. Teresa added, "Then I shall only have scorn and disdain for all the demons, for they will be afraid of me. I do not understand those who cry out in fear, the devil! the devil! when we can say God! God!"

And so, confidence in our interior Guests brings us safety in temptation. For, unless we ourselves will it, no temptation is able to tear us away from God. "Who shall separate us from the love of Christ? For in all these things we are more than conquerors because of Him who has loved us. For I am sure that neither death nor life, nor angels, nor principalities . . . nor any other creature shall be able to separate us from the love of God, which is in Christ Jesus our Lord" (Romans 8:35, 37, 38, 39).

The Lord is my light and my salvation.
Whom shall I fear?
The Lord is the stronghold of my life;
of Whom shall I be afraid?

When evildoers assail me, uttering slanders
against me, my adversaries and foes, they shall
stumble and fall.
For He will hide me in His shelter in the day
of trouble.

He will set me high upon a rock.
Shall not my soul be subject to God?
For from Him is my salvation.
He is my God and my Saviour.
My Protector, I shall be moved no more.

Psalms 27; 62

5. Union in Bodily Suffering

Suffering is necessary. It is written of our Master, "It was necessary for Christ to suffer..." (Luke 24:46). It is true also of His followers, "All that will live godly in Jesus Christ will suffer persecution" (2 Timothy 3:12). We must ascend to Heaven as Christ ascended Calvary carrying the Cross. "If any man will follow Me, let him deny himself and take up his cross and follow Me" (Mark 8:34).

Thus, it is essential to know how to suffer.

All suffering is not good. Sometimes it is useless; sometimes even harmful. Even some good people have a morbid tendency to seek suffering in itself—to desire it and find pleasure in it. They act contrary to the designs of God—forgetting that suffering is never an end in itself, but always a means. It is one of the sources of love. The interior disposition of the sufferer is that which makes suffering holy and meritorious. Suffering is not the work of God, but the result of sin. If love did not penetrate it, making it fruitful to our fallen nature, it would remain definitely harmful.

On Calvary, a thief was crucified on each side of Christ. To one, his pangs opened Paradise; to the other, they were the prelude of eternal suffering.

Thus, it is not so much a question of suffering, but of suffering well—of doing so in conformity with the divine will. It involves suffering with Christ as Christ suffered.

On the royal way of the Cross, we have three stages to pass through: bodily suffering, grief of heart, and desolation of soul.

In bodily suffering, first of all, we must follow St. Paul's advice, "Present your bodies as a living sacrifice—holy and pleasing unto God" (Romans 12:1).

Suffering attacks primarily the body and the lower faculties of the soul; grief, in the strict sense of the term, strikes the affections of the heart. Suffering is the Christian's primary and fundamental participation in the Passion of Christ. At times, however, it may reach an elevated degree. For there are some bodily sufferings and infirmities which are very hard for nature to bear. And these may both glorify God and be meritorious for the soul.

On the road of bodily suffering, Jesus has gone before us. Indeed, He has gone far beyond our capability of following Him. Because He came with Calvary in view, the Holy Spirit specially strengthened His humanity to bear pain. At the same time, the Spirit endowed Him with an exquisite sensibility, so that He would be capable of suffering to excess. His capacity for suffering was increased to an extraordinary extent by the very perfection of His humanness. His Passion was a true overflowing of torture and pain. Isaiah scarcely knew how to describe it:

He was despised and rejected by men,
    a man of sorrows and acquainted with grief.
And as one from whom men hide their faces,
    He was despised, and we esteemed him not. . . .
He had no form or comeliness in him that we
    should look at him;
    and no beauty that we should desire him. . . .
Yet it was the will of the Lord to bruise him. . . .

                        Isaiah 53

What must we do, then, when suffering comes? We must unite ourselves closely to Him who has suffered so much! This is at the same time the easiest and most helpful method, for we can remind ourselves that we are members of Christ. This implies that we must continue His Passion, participating in both the sufferings and wounds of His divine body. Today, His glory, which has been purchased at such a price, makes it impossible for Him to suffer further. However, He wishes that what His human nature can no longer undergo should be endured by his mystical body, thereby continuing His passion in us.

Even more: doesn't it now seem that He wishes to continue in us the humiliations of that Passion, just because His perfections kept Him from doing so completely? Undoubtedly, He suffered during His mortal life more than we would even be capable of doing. However, there were aspects of suffering which He was unable to experience—illness, for example. What He Himself did not bear, He bears now in us. He enters our life—incorporating Himself with us, so that we may be able to suffer not only for Him, but with and in Him. Thus we may truly say, "With Christ I am nailed to the Cross" (Galations 2:19).

All suffering well borne hastens the work of God in us. Nothing is more sanctifying. It gives us an intimate likeness to Jesus, that marvellous work which St. Paul terms "the formation of Christ in us" (cf Galatians 4: 19). . . . "Though our outer nature is wasting away, our inner nature is being renewed every day" (2 Corinthians 4:16). "Each pain," said Monsignor Gay, "is a kiss of the crucifix increasing our likeness to Jesus."

Supported in such a way, shall we not bear the worst sufferings with patience and holy joy? "With all my affliction, I am overjoyed" (2 Corinthians 7:4), said St. Paul. "Now I rejoice in my sufferings for your sake, and in my flesh I complete what is lacking in Christ's afflictions for the sake of His body—that is, the church . . ." (Colossians 1:24).

He congratulated those Christians who were especially tried in the following words, "For it has been granted to you that, for the sake of Christ, you should not only believe in Him, but also suffer for His sake. . . ." (Philippians 1:29).*

Our aim, therefore, must be to suffer with Jesus as our close companion. Thus, we shall make our own those words of the great Apostle:

> We are afflicted in every way, but not crushed;
>   perplexed, but not driven to despair;
>   persecuted, but not forsaken, struck down,
>   but not destroyed;
> always carrying in the body the death of Jesus,
>   so that the life of Jesus may also be manifested

---

*Mother Margaret Mary Doens, suffering from a long and terrible illness, seemed to rejoice in her pain. "One could almost believe that you are enjoying yourself," said one of her sisters. "Yes," she replied, "I am happy because Our Lord does what He pleases with me. . . ."

in our bodies.
For, while we live,
    we are always being given up to death
    for Jesus' sake,
    so that the life of Jesus may be manifested
        in our mortal flesh. . . .
For, this slight momentary affliction
    is preparing for us
    an eternal weight of glory beyond
    all comparison. . . ."

    2 Corinthians 4:8-11, 17

O my Lord Jesus, I believe, and by Thy grace will ever believe and hold, and I know that it is true, and will be true to the end of the world, that nothing great is done without suffering, without humiliation, and that all things are possible by means of it.

I believe, O my God, that poverty is better than riches, pain better than pleasure, obscurity and contempt than name, and ignomony and reproach than honour.

My Lord, I do not ask thee to bring these trials on me, for I know not if I could face them. But at least, O Lord, whether I be in prosperity or adversity, I will believe that it is as I have said.

I will never have faith in riches, rank, power, or reputation. I will never set my heart on worldly success, or on worldly advantages. I will never wish for what men call the prizes of life.

I will ever, with Thy grace, make much of those who are despised and neglected, honour the poor, revere the suffering and admire and venerate Thy saints and confessors, and take my part with them in spite of the world.

And lastly, O my dear Lord, though I am so very weak that I am not fit to ask for suffering as a gift, and have not the strength to do so, at least I will beg of Thee grace to meet suffering well, when Thou in Thy love and wisdom dost bring it upon me. . . .

I wish to humble myself in all things, and to be silent when I am ill-used, and to be patient when sorrow or pain is prolonged, and all for the love of Thee and Thy Cross, knowing that in this way I shall gain the promise both of this life and the next.

Cardinal Newman

6. Union in Grief of Heart

The second stage is grief of heart. This is very different in its causes and modes of action. Grief directly attacks the heart: disappointments, weariness, separations, discords, profound sadness. Grief is more trying to nature, and at the same time more purifying, because it calls for greater renunciation. Thereby, it produces a more elevated sanctity. We share more fully in the Passion of Christ by grief than by pain. The bodily sufferings of Our Lord were undoubtedly intense. But, who could accurately estimate the depths of His grief and the agony of His heart? Because His heart was an abyss of love, it was also an abyss of grief. We know the Isaian title which has been applied to Christ: "The man of sorrows." His life was indeed one long sorrow occasioned by His knowledge, His holiness, and His infinite love. Grief and sorrow, beginning at the Incarnation, reached their climax during His Passion. His was an unutterable martyrdom for thirty-three years, filling to the full His capacity for suffering. "He lived continually with grief," said

Blessed Angela of Foligno. Whoever aspires to perfect union must enter courageously into the grief of Christ, bearing with Him disappointments, slanders, and agony of heart. It was St. Paul's desire "That I may know Him . . . and the fellowship of His sufferings, becoming like Him in His death." (Philippians 3:10).

Thus the believer, whatever his anguish (even though it may seem so extreme as to be incapable of any relief), may still dwell with God. For always before him he will find Jesus bearing a like burden, suffering a similar agony (and even harder trials), which He sanctifies and deifies. Dwelling thus with Him in grief of heart, the believer also dwells together with Him in love.

> Why art thou sad, O my soul,
>> and why dost thou trouble me?
> Hope in God, for I will still praise Him,
>> the salvation of my countenance and my God.
> Give us help in trouble,
>> for vain is the help of man.
> Through God we shall do mighty things,
>> and He will bring our enemies to nothing.
> The mercies of the Lord
>> I will sing forever!

Psalms 42, 108, 89

7. Union in Desolation of Soul

At certain times, it almost seems as if God were taking sides against us, and we endure terrible combats. These periodic desolations are the greatest trials of all which He sends us. They are also the most rare, for the majority of souls are incapable of knowing them. Nevertheless, we could say that it is desolations which add the "finishing touch" to the soul's development.

At the same time that it tests and tries love, suffering also results in the satisfaction of divine justice. Desolations mark on the soul the stamp of perfection; they imprint upon it the closest likeness to Christ.

They proceed directly from God. Their source is His infinite holiness; their immediate case is the mysterious and awesome work of the Holy Spirit, who desires to make the soul participate in the eternal and sovereign Purity. For the sake of this end, it is seized, ravaged, broken, abandoned, and seized again. It is plunged into bitterness and tested by a thousand trials until transformation is complete. It is God Himself who is acting in this way without any intermediary, in order that He might attain access to the secret depths of the soul. He wishes to penetrate into the very root of the spirit and into all the intricacies of the heart.

> For the word of God is living and active, sharper than any two-edged sword, piercing to the division of soul and spirit, of joints and marrow, and discerning the thoughts and intentions of the heart.
>
> Hebrews 4:12

At times like this, everything is painful—even the thought of graces formerly received. This is on account of the secret and most pure light which the Holy Spirit diffuses in the soul. On the one hand, this light manifests the greatness of God; on the other, it reveals our own misery and nothingness. Thus, it casts everything else into an intense gloom, destroys all natural consolations, and establishes a desolate solitude in the presence of the Most Holy. Thus, the soul is plunged into a terrible spiritual darkness, even into a condition of terror and anguish. In this manner, God purifies the soul completely, for "our God is a consuming fire . . ." (Hebrews 12:29).

What, then, are we to do? Freely surrendering to God and to His divine action is the only course; any other would be harmful, not to say impossible. Since it is the Holy Spirit Himself who acts, to dwell in this purifying desolation is to dwell with God.

Union with Christ in His Passion is then more useful than ever. However, great our desolation may be, it can never approach the absolute desolation of Christ Himself when, during those terrible hours, there were wrung from Him the words, "My soul is sorrowful, even unto death...." "My God, My God, why hast thou forsaken me?" (Matthew 26:38; 27:46). Here, we see God the Father "letting loose against His well-beloved Son all the powers of hell, seeming at the same time to withdraw from Him all the protection of heaven" (Bossuet).

Under such conditions, the union of the soul with Jesus, usually so sweet and consoling, is frozen up, as it were; there is no word of consolation. The heart *feels* absolutely nothing. It lives only by faith. It is in faith that the soul must unite and, in some measure, fasten itself on God. Faith is the only refuge, the "immovable kingdom" (Hebrews 12:28), of which St. Paul says "in faith you stand" (2 Corinthians 1:23).

More than ever, the afflicted soul must believe without the slightest wavering in God's "exceeding charity" (Ephesians 2:4), imitating Moses whose unshaken faith "endured as seeing Him who is invisible" (Hebrews 11:27). The soul must also believe that God never loved her so much, nor was ever so close to her, as in those moments when He appeared to repulse her. "The more that you think you are abandoned," said Our Lord to Blessed Angela of Foligno, "the more you are beloved and drawn towards Me. . . . O my well-beloved, know that in this state there is between God and yourself the most intimate union." And so, let us remember the words of St. John, "We believe the love which God has for us" (1 John 4:16).

In these terrible, but blessed, hours of interior desolation, or rather of supernatural purification, great things are accomplished. Love consummates the union of the soul with God according to His promise, "I will espouse thee to me in faithfulness" (Hosea 2:20). Then, with the work of purification accomplished, the spouse appears re-clad with strength, purity, and joy: "Who is this that comes up from the wilderness, leaning upon her beloved, flowing with delights?"* (Canticles 8:5).

In summary: during these trials, there is only one thing that we can really do: We must keep ourselves firmly united to Jesus, and by the wounds of His sacred humanity she will penetrate to the Divinity.

The soul must be offered up as a holocaust. When we consent, this holocaust is not only united with that of Jesus. But, even more, He makes it His own. With Jesus, the soul comes before God as one glorious holocaust. Then the whole Trinity looks upon the soul with pleasure: when the Father recognized in her the features of His beloved Son, He pours out on her His tenderest affection. When the Word sees her following His passion, he accepts her as His spouse. The Holy Spirit loves in her the perfect instrument of His grace for the sanctification of the Church, and thus He makes Himself her inspirer and guide.

And so, let us not complain of suffering. Rather, we should embrace the Cross with the same readiness as Jesus, who offered Himself as a "sacrifice to God for an odour of sweetness" (Ephesians 5:2).

"If jealousy could ever enter into the realms of eternal love," said St. Francis de Sales, "the angels would

---

*"What will you do, O spouse of Christ? Do you wish to penetrate that holy and sacred sanctuary, where one may see the Son in the Father and the Father in the Son? Do you wish to dwell with the Holy Trinity? You can do so IF YOU HAVE FAITH. FOR ALL THINGS ARE POSSIBLE TO HIM WHO BELIEVES. What will Faith not find for You? It attains the inaccessible, discovers the unknown, embraces the immense. Open your heart, for it enshrines the Eternal."

St. Bernard, Serm. 76 in Cant.

envy the sufferings of God for man, and those of man for God."

Blessed is the pain, and blessed is the death, which enables us to say with the Apostle, "I have been crucified with Christ. It is no longer I who live, but Christ who lives in me. And the life I now live in the flesh, I live by faith in the Son of God, who loved me and gave himself for me . . . " (Galatians 2:19, 20).

> *Save me, O God!*
>> *For the waters have come up to my neck.*
> *I sink in deep waters (mire),*
>> *where there is no foothold.*
> *I have come into deep waters,*
>> *and the flood sweeps over me.*
> *I am weary with crying,*
>> *my throat is parched.*
> *My eyes grow dim*
>> *with waiting for my God.*

Psalm 69

> *Bless the Lord, O my soul,*
>> *and forget not all His benefits.*
> *Bless the Lord, O my soul,*
>> *and all that is within me bless His holy name.*
> *He forgives all your iniquities,*
>> *he heals all your diseases.*
> *He redeems your life from the Pit,*
>> *and crowns you with steadfast*
>> *love and mercy. . . .*

Psalm 103

8. Union in Joy

It is of great importance to watch over our joys. What is joy—if not the gladness of the soul in the possession of what it loves? The nature of our joy manifests the nature of our love; the purity of our heart reflects its purity. We must then take great care that our joys do not lead us away from God. We must take St. Paul's advice, "Let this mind be in you which was also in Christ Jesus" (Philippians 2:5). Rejoice with Jesus; but rejoice with Him only in those things in ourselves or in our neighbour which would make Him glad.

In all things, we should keep ourselves especially close to Jesus—but especially in our joys and our love.

a. The Source of Joy

Joy comes to us from creatures. Some of these joys are most pleasurable—for example, the joy of friendship. Since they come from God, we are not forbidden to enjoy them. However, we should take care that they lead back to God. Let us not love anything outside of Him. Rather, let us love all creatures with Him

—and as He loves them. We must love all things *in* Him. This union with God will make our joys pure and eminently free.

However, joys such as these are only secondary. The basic joy for the Christian is to know that *God is*. God exists! It is to know that there is the infinite, the essential and necessary Being, the cause of all, truth, beauty, goodness, benevolence, power, holiness, sovereign purity, justice, and love . . . God exists. He is all that! Eternally, unchangeably, infinitely, He is all that! He knows and loves Himself. He is One, and He is Three: the Father, Word, and Spirit. As Father, He opens out His infinite Life in His Son, who is His thought and glory. These two consummate themselves in the unity of their common love: the Holy Spirit. He is the fundamental and eternal term of their mysterious embrace, their joy, their infinite happiness. The Father, Son, and Spirit love themselves with a love without measure. They are infinitely and unchangeably happy forever . . .

And they call us to communicate forever in their life. To know this is a source of supreme and unending joy for the loving soul. To rejoice that God is God, to rejoice in God's own joy, is a supremely holy and sublime act. It is pure charity. This joy detaches our soul from the miseries of our poor human life to raise it above all, making it enter into the intimate life of the holy Trinity. This is equivalent to what St. Paul terms "the deep things of God" (1 Corinthians 2:10). It is one of the more divine fruits of the presence and operation of the Holy Spirit in the redeemed soul. It deifies the soul. To this one joy all the rest should be referred. This will be easy if we remember that all our joys are (and cannot be anything but), a gushing forth from that infinite joy of the Holy Spirit "who is given us" (Romans 5:5).

The source of all joy is in us: "He who believes in me, as the Scripture says, 'Out of his heart shall flow fountains of living water.'" The evangelist then adds that Jesus said this "about the Spirit, which those who believed in him were to receive" (John 7:38-39). Baptism opened for us this interior source, and each interior communion augments it. "There is a river whose streams make glad the city of God, the holy habitation of the Most High" (Psalm 46:4).

The smallest truth of faith is a world of joy which our heart can constantly taste. "Though you do not now see Him, you believe in Him and rejoice with unutterable and exalted joy" (1 Peter 1:8), said the Prince of the Apostles. And Isaiah adds, "You shall be like a watered garden and like a fountain whose springs never fail" (Isaiah 58:11).

Thus, it depends on us to live in joy. And what joy! There are pure and true human joys, but they move only over the surface of the soul. Divine joys penetrate to its very center. Yes: true joy, essential joy that cannot be taken from us, wells up from the *presence in us* of the blessed Trinity. Once we know ourselves thus enfolded with the divine, what can really trouble the peace and interrupt the harmony of our souls?

b. *To Live in Joy*

"Rejoice in the Lord always; again I say, rejoice" (Philippians 4:4). God has created His children for joy. He has done everything so that they might live in Joy. What is creation, what is sanctification, if not either natural or supernatural happiness—an effusion of the divine joy? What is the Eucharist, if not an inexhaustible source of joy, open in the Church and in each soul? God wishes that we live in joy. Jesus asked for this in His last prayer. "Father, I pray that My joy may be in them, and their Joy fulfilled" (John 17:13).

Even sorrow should be changed and converted into joy. Christ's soul contained both immense joys and immense sorrows at the same moment. Its depths were plunged into anguish, while the heights were filled with divine happiness. Yet, joy dominated; it came to dissolve all His sufferings and sacrifices. For Jesus knew that the heavier these were, the more they glorified God and prepared a loftier exaltation for His humanity.

Our soul, too, can be both desolate and joyous. It can be desolate in its inferior part, which approaches the sense. It can be joyous at those heights which alone govern the will. Even in those hours when sorrow seems to hold sway, we have within us the One who consoles. "I will ask the Father. And he shall give you another Comforter, that He may abide with you for ever. The Spirit of Truth. . . . And He shall be in you" (John 14:16, 17).

Let us dwell in joy, for this will be to dwell in the Holy Spirit. We should remember that Holy Communion plunges us into Him whom St. Catherine called the "ocean of peace." "O Eternal God," she cried, "You are the tranquil ocean in which souls live and are nourished. They find repose in the union of love."

Joy is a worship to give to God. It is the barometer of the soul: its degree indicates the degree of love. Amidst her perpetual difficulties and persecutions, the Church as the sublime type of the soul never ceases to rejoice. Her liturgy is a fête beginning anew each day. She counts her days by the feasts. She marches in sorrow, but her eyes are raised to the heavens singing the perfection and love of her Spouse. She lives in joy—a joy free, serene, and strong, the fruit of love.

The Christian is a sower of joy; that is why he does great things. For joy is one of the irresistible powers of the world: it pacifies, conquers, disarms, and draws to itself. The joyous soul is an apostle, drawing men to God. It manifests everything which God's presence brings about. This is why the Holy Spirit gives the counsel, "Do not be sad, for the joy of the Lord is our strength" (2 Esdras 8:10).

Joy and gladness be to You,
 in my name O God of my life,
 for the sovereignty of the Trinity,
 the essential unity of your substance,
 the distinction of Your persons,
 for their union and intimate relations
 as the source of Your ineffable joy.

Joy and gladness be to You
 for Your incomprehensible grandeur,
 Your unchanging eternity,
 Your supreme holiness,
  which excludes all stain
  and is the source of all purity,
 and for Your glorious and perfect happiness.

Joy and gladness be to You
 for the very pure flesh of Your humanity
  by which You have purified me,
 for Your most sacred soul,
 for Your divine heart,
  which was pierced by me even to death.

Joy and gladness be to You

in that true loving heart
so filled with solicitude for me,
so thirsty in its love for me,
that it will never repose until it receives me
into itself for eternity.

Joy and gladness be to You
for the most worthy heart and soul
of the glorious Virgin Mary, Your Mother,
whom You have given me as Mother
in the difficulties of my salvation,
and who is always opening for me the treasures
of her maternal solicitude.

Joy and gladness be to You
from all your creatures
which fill the heavens, the earth,
and the abyss.
May they give you that eternal praise
which, issuing from You as its source,
remounts thither again.

Joy and gladness be to You
from my heart and soul,
my spirit and my flesh,
and from all created beings.

To You,
by Whom and in Whom are all things,
to You be honour and glory
for all eternity! . . .

                                        St. Gertrude

B. TO PERFECT UNION

Union with God by the state of sanctifying grace can exist in many degrees. On the scale of perfection, the degrees are almost infinite. Each morning, Communion establishes in us a union of love which we have tried to describe. Unfortunately, this union can be destroyed. Yet, on the other hand, it can always become more perfect. Our efforts throughout the day should strive to augment and perfect this eucharistic union. A very useful means of doing so is by the repetition of acts of love and desire.

1. Repetition of Acts of Desire

Daniel was given a knowledge of the mystery of Christ because he was a *man of desires*. A soul who really desires Jesus cannot help entering deeply into the knowledge and appreciation of His mysteries.

Desire removes obstacles and opens the door of the soul, so that those poignant words of the Apocalypse are realized: "Behold, I stand at the door and knock. If any one hears my voice and opens the door, I will come in to him and sup with him, and he with me" (Apocalypse 3:20).

Desire dilates the soul and makes it ready for the object of its desires; in some measure, it makes the soul equivalent to God. The heavenly Father deigned to say to St. Catherine of Siena: "No virtue can merit eternal life for you if you serve Me in a finite manner, for I the infinite God wish to be served in an infinite manner, and you have nothing approaching the infinite—except the desire and transports of your soul." However, He said again, "this desire, as in the case of all the other virtues, is of value only through Christ crucified, my only Son" (St. Catherine of Siena, Dialogue 4 and 92).

It is most useful to arouse in the soul a longing for Communion. "The perfect exercise of love," says Bossuet, "is to desire without ceasing to receive Jesus Christ. The table is prepared, the guests lack, although Jesus calls them."

The life of many of the saints has been one long and ardent aspiration of their soul towards the eucharistic union. The martyr St. Ignatius wrote to the Romans, "I do not desire the pleasures of this world, but I do desire the bread of God, the bread of heaven, the bread of life, the flesh of Christ the Son of the living God. I yearn to be inebriated with that beverage which is His blood, which lights up in us an incorruptible love, the pledge of eternal life."

St. Catherine of Siena longed night and day after Communion. As soon as it was dawn, she hastened to the Church, literally borne there by the desire which gave strength to her exhausted body. She often said to Blessed Raymond, in order to express her desire for Communion, "Father, I am very hungry. Give my soul its nourishment."

"My heart feels consumed with the desire to love my God," said St. Margaret Mary, "and this gives me an insatiable desire for Communion, and for suffering. . . ." One Good Friday, having an ardent desire to receive Our Lord, she recounts: "I said to Him tearfully, 'O most loved Jesus, I really long for You. And although I am not able to receive You today, I do not cease to desire You.' He then came to console me with His sweet presence and said, 'My daughter, your desire has touched My heart so much that, if I had not already instituted this sacrament of love, I would right now in order to make Myself your food. I take so much delight in being desired that, as often as the heart makes this wish, this often do I see her with love and draw her to Me.' "

Jesus now repeats from the Tabernacle the same invitation as when formerly He stood and cried to the crowd under the porticoes of the Temple, "If any man thirst, let him come to Me and drink" (John 7:37). Or, renewing the invitation of Divine Wisdom, "Come to me, all you who desire me, and be filled with my fruits" (Sirach 14:26).

Thus, let us try to arouse in ourselves more frequent and ardent desires, so that our soul may be constantly turned towards the Eucharist. We should live in that state of desire and aspiration depicted by the psalmist, "With open mouth I pant, because I long for Thy commandments" (Psalm 118:131). This thirst for the divine is one of the precious graces of God foretold by the Prophets, "Behold, the days are coming," says the Lord God, "when I will send a famine on the land: not a famine of bread, nor a thirst for water, but of hearing the words of the Lord" (Amos 8:11).

How far may our desires reach? Can we aspire to the more secret mysteries of divine union?

Yes—provided that our desire is humble, and joyfully submissive to God's will.

It would doubtless be foolish pride (and it would also place us under the worst illusions) if we were to desire extraordinary favors—such as the graces *"gratis datae"* (revelations, visions, etc.,). However, to desire the closest possible union of our soul with God is both legitimate and praiseworthy. "O that He would kiss me with the kisses of His mouth," (Song of Solomon

1:1), cries the spouse of the Canticle. And she speaks for all who, bought and sanctified by grace, aspire to that condition of soul where "he who is joined to the Lord is one spirit" (1 Corinthians 6:17). Who makes the barren soil of our souls bring forth such holy and daring desires? The Holy Spirit Himself. . . . *He* it is who orients our soul towards God. "For we do not know how to pray as we ought. But the Spirit Himself intercedes for us with sighs too deep for words;" it is He through whom we cry "Abba, Father" (Romans 8: 15, 26). A most excellent means both to stimulate and express our desire for God is to make use of Scripture and borrow from it those words which have so often expressed the need for God:

> As a deer longs for flowing streams,
>   So longs my soul for thee, O God.
> My soul thirsts for God, for the living God . . .
> O God, You are my God, I seek thee.
>   My soul thirsts for thee . . .
> as in a dry and weary land, where no water is . . .
>
> Psalms 42 and 63

2. Repetition of Acts of Love

St. John wrote "God is love" (1 John 4:8). We can also say Jesus is love. And we should also be able to add that the Christian is love. Within the blessed Trinity, the life of the Word consists of loving His Father—flowing towards Him again and again with an immense love, returning to Him all that He has received.

Love was also His life while on earth. The Word became incarnate for love of His Father, in order to reveal Him for us and to win us for Him. Love both made Him man and nailed Him to the Cross. Behind all His mysteries, beneath all His works and sufferings, there is the love of His Father, "I live by the Father" (John 6:58). It is this same love which has made Him become bread for us, thereby retaining Him in the silence of the Tabernacle. What does He do in the impenetrable silence of the Host? Above all, He loves His Father. The communicant who seeks to live like Jesus will, in the first place, love God. He will love Him as the First Commandment requires: *with all his heart, all his soul, and all his strength*. It is undoubtedly impossible for weak human nature to continually create specific acts of love. But we can (with God's grace) so multiply them that they dominate the activities of our other faculties, thereby exercising on our life an influence which becomes constantly closer and more penetrating.

To make an act of charity is so easy. A simple movement of the heart is enough. The humblest action, the last sacrifice, can be transformed into an act of love. "All that is done for love *is* love," said St. Francis de Sales. "Work, fatigue, and even death are love when they are undergone for love. As Pére Lacordaire tells us, "the love of God is the supreme act of the soul, the highest action of man." "The smallest act of pure love," adds St. John of the Cross, "has more value in God's eyes than all the other acts united."

"There is nothing in the world so real, so substantial, as the love of God. In comparison with this great reality, all the rest is a wan shadow. Everything else is empty and soon will vanish. An act of love is a complete work. Its effects are more powerful, more important, than the effects and consequences of all other acts. Death itself cannot equal it in grandeur. And yet, what constitutes an act of love? It is a simple movement of the heart which, as swiftly as lightning, penetrates the heavens. Such acts may be multiplied beyond all calculations, even amidst the most distracting occupations. Far from being enfeebled by repetition, they derive from it a new intensity and an unknown power. Not only do they require no effort. But it is also a pleasure for us to formulate them" (Faber).

"Those who desire to love ardently," says St. Francis de Sales, "will soon love with ardour." So, let us not cease to love! "Ah! if I had a thousand hearts to love

with," exclaimed St. Margaret Mary, "that would not
be too much." St. Paul tells us that love is not only the
purpose of the commandments, but also the 'fulfilling of the law" (Romans 13:10). Just as love gives God
to the creature, love also gives the creature to God,
thereby achieving their union. Love makes them one.
And, after having joined them together, Love makes
them rest there. "He who abides in love abides in
God, and God in him . . ." (1 John 4:16).

"It is of the greatest importance," says St. John of
the Cross, "that the soul exercises itself much in love,
so that it can accomplish its course rapidly. In that
way, it is not detained here below, but soon arrives to
see God face-to-face."

"The assiduous exercise of love," he said again, "is a
great thing. The soul arrives at perfection, and the
consummation of love cannot be long delayed—
whether in this life or the next—without seeing the
face of God" (Spiritual maxims).

> My God, my love, You are all mine,
>   and I am all Yours.
> Fill me with love, so that I may taste
>   in my inmost heart
> how sweet it is to love, to be dissolved and
>   absorbed by love.
> May love ravish me, and raise me above myself
>   by its transports.
> May I chant the canticle of love,
>   May I follow You,
> my best Beloved, to the heights of Your glory.
> May all the strength of my soul
>   be expended in praising
> and loving You. May I love You more than myself,

and may I love myself only for You.
May I love in You all who truly love You,
   as it is ordained in the law of Love which
from You shines forth.

Imitation, Book III, Ch. V.

3. The Invisible Divine Missions

Here is a truth capable of arousing the soul to great desires and inspiring an intense love.

We know that theology considers the Invisible Divine Missions as amongst the profound mysteries of religion. They are new divine outpourings. They are fresh illuminations that the Word communicates to our intelligence. They are renewed impulses of love with which the Holy Spirit fills our wills. They resemble and are an extension of the eternal processions of the Son and the Holy Spirit.

Each time that a soul, through its fervour and generosity, makes new progress in the love of God and merits a new grace, the Father sends to this soul the Word and the Holy Spirit. These, in turn, bring new rights to the divine intimacy. And since the three persons are inseparable, the Father comes without being sent. The Three Persons flood the soul with a new influx of life, and a new relationship is established which is more personal, real, and intimate than that of the moment previously. This wonderful mystery can be reproduced at each moment. And, with every increase of love, there is an invisible visit of "The Three." Every moment, then, that the soul increases its charity, the blessed Trinity flows into it, bringing fresh floods of light and love. By means of these mysterious elevations, is there any limit to the height the soul can ascend?

O Christian, *if only you knew the gift of God!* (cf John 4:10).

O Trinity, most High, most merciful
and bountiful God,
Father, Son, and Holy Spirit,
One God I hope in You.
Instruct, direct, sustain me.

O Father! by Your infinite power,
fill and fix in my memory
holy and divine thoughts.

O Son! By Your eternal Wisdom,
enlighten my understanding.
Grant me knowledge of Your supreme truth
and my own nothingness.

O Holy Spirit! Who are the love of the Father and
the Son! By Your incomprehensible goodness,
unite my will to Yours and enkindle it
with the flame of Your love.

O my Lord and my God! My beginning and end,
O Essence supremely simple,
tranquil and lovable.
O abyss of sweetness and all delights!
O most loved light and the supreme good
of my soul!
Inexpressible ocean of joy,

and perfect fulness of all good!
My God and my all, what will it be
    when I shall possess You?

You are my unique and unchangeable good.
You alone do I seek.
You alone I desire, for you alone do I search.
Lord, draw me to Yourself.
I knock, O Lord,—open to me.
    Open to one forsaken who implores You.
Into the abyss of your divinity,
    plunge me.
Make me one sole spirit with You,
    so that I may possess *within me*
    Your treasures.

St. Albert the Great

VI. THE END OF THE EUCHARISTIC UNION

+A. ADOPTED SONS IN JESUS CHRIST
+1. Our supernatural vocation and the Trinity.
+2. Communion and our supernatural vocation

ıB. THE GLORY OF THE MOST HOLY TRINITY
+1. The supreme end of creation
+2. The unique Liturgy

VI. THE END OF THE EUCHARISTIC UNION

A. Adopted Sons in Jesus Christ

1. Our Supernatural Vocation and the Trinity

"Blessed be the God and Father of our Lord Jesus Christ . . . even as he chose us in him before the foundation of the world, that we should be holy and blameless before him. He destined us in love to be His sons. . . ." (Ephesians 1:3, 4). Thus, God has concerned Himself with us from all eternity. The Father thought of us, and this thought was at the same time a volition. For each of us He uttered a word which created us, expresses us, and contains our temporal and external life. It ordained what we should become, the place we should occupy, the perfection we should realize, and the glory we ought to attain. Interpreting His supreme thought in relation to us, the Father pronounced this word when He established our supernatural vocation. This Word is the supreme law and the outline of our existence. And it indicates in what measure we shall enter into the divine creative plan.

Apart from this thought, the Father does not know

us with a knowledge of love. He occupies Himself with us, giving us grace. He gives Himself only as far as we move in the light of His thought. And it is through the realization of this that we enter into the divine order of eternal realities.

Our basic duty thus reduces itself to this: the accomplishment of our Heavenly Father's will. This means living according to the Word He has pronounced about us, accepting in advance all this word entails (whether of joy or of sorrow). In short: this means submitting ourselves lovingly to all His demands as they are manifested in our daily lives. But what *is* this mysterious thought? Who said this word? St. Paul replies, "Those whom He foreknew he also predestined to be conformable to the image of His Son . . ." (Romans 8:29). God's will is that we shall enter into the mystery of Christ. The word He pronounces over us expresses the manner and measure in which we should reproduce Jesus for the glory of our Heavenly Father. "He chose us before the foundation of the world. . . . He destined us in love to be His Sons through Jesus Christ, according to the purpose of His Will, to the praise of His glorious grace which He freely bestowed on us in the Beloved. . . ." (Ephesians 1:4, 5, 6).

Such is our supernatural vocation: to be conformed to Jesus, live like Jesus, become like Jesus.

The incarnate Word is the unique and universal ideal which all those who are predestined by love should represent and manifest: scholars, priests, religious, celibate, or married. For everyone there is only one example: Jesus Christ Himself, whom they are bound to imitate under penalty of being excluded from the realm of grace. The measure of their perfection or their supernatural fruitfulness will correspond exactly to the measure of their adherence to Jesus, as well as their faithful resemblance to Him. "And there is salvation in no one else...." (Acts 4:12).

To what extent should I reproduce this? I do not know. That is the very mysterious secret of eternal predestination. But certainly, I ought to reproduce it. I ought without ceasing to look at Jesus, imitate Jesus, become Jesus.

How can one accomplish such a sublime vocation? Through grace and with the co-operation of the Holy Spirit, "to be with you forever" (John 14:16). The Holy Spirit makes Himself the executor of the designs of the Father, the artisan of man's dedication, which the Father traced on the model of the Word Incarnate. *Digitus paternae dexternae*, sings the Church. "You, O creative Spirit, are the finger of God the Father" (Hymn: "Veni Creator"). As the painter or sculptor expresses through his handiwork the ideal he has conceived, so the heavenly Father inscribes and engraves in us His image the word. He does this by means of the Holy Spirit, in order to translate His thought.

The first work of this creative and sanctifying spirit in us is to transform us into the resemblance of the Son of God, and to make us live in conformity with our divine sonship. "For all who are led by the Spirit of God are Sons of God. For you did not receive the spirit of slavery to fall back into fear, but you have received the spirit of sonship. When we cry 'Abba! Father!' it is the Spirit Himself bearing witness with our spirit that we are children of God, and if children, then heirs—heirs of God and fellow heirs with Christ, provided we suffer with Him in order that we may also be glorified with Him. . . ." (Romans 8:14-17).

The spirit of truth will illumine in our soul the eternal thought of the Father. By revealing Jesus in us, He will make it clearer and more precise—as well as more attractive. "When the Spirit of Truth comes, he will guide you into all the truth . . . He will glorify me . . ." (John 16:13, 14).

Being the consummation and the consecration of all things, He continues to impress in our soul that adorable thought of the Father which is Jesus. He fixes it, makes it permanent—and, if we wish, irrevocable. This was the mystery which David contemplated when he sang, "Lift up the light of thy countenance upon us, O Lord" (Ps 4:7). For the likeness of the Lord —His splendour and His glory—is the Word.

Afterwards, because He is the Spirit of Life and the author of supernatural life, He is the realization of the Father's thought. He also stimulates us to resemble Christ more closely. And He helps us until we are all formed into "mature manhood, to the measure of the stature of the fulness of Christ . . . until Christ be formed in (us)" (Ephesians 4:13; Galatians 4:19).

Finally, since He Himself is love personally, He establishes relations of love between us and the Trinity. Also, He creates a constant tendency towards Union. He draws the Trinity towards us, and us towards the Trinity. He is the constant appeal, the living attraction, and the irresistible impulse which draws us to Jesus— so much so that, in the measure the soul abandons itself to the Father's thought with the Holy Spirit's help, the union becomes closer and closer. And as the Father is in the Son and the Son in the Father, so the soul is in Christ and Christ is in the soul. According to the prayer at the Last Supper, the "two are made perfect in one" (John 17:23).

Then, ransomed and sanctified, man may present himself confidently before the Heavenly Father and say to Him, "Do not turn away the face of thy anointed one . . ." (Psalm 132:10).

> O eternal Trinity! You are an unfathomable sea,
>   wherein the more I plunge,
>   the more I find You.
> And the more I find You,
>   the more I seek you again.
> Of You it can never be said: "It is enough!"
> The soul which satiates itself in Your depths
>   still desires You unceasingly
>   because it still hungers for You.
> Eternal Trinity, the soul aways wishes to see light
>   by Your Light.
> As the deer thirsts after flowing streams,
>   so my soul longs to depart
>   from the dark prison of my body
>   to truly see You. . . .
>
> O eternal divinity! Ocean without limit.
>   Could You do more than to give me Yourself?
> You are the ever-burning fire
>   which is never extinguished.
>   You are the fire which consumes in itself
>   all the self-love of the soul
> You are the fire which melts and lights,
>   and by whose Light
>   You have made known to me the truth.
> You are the light of all lights. . . .
>
> O supreme and infinite Good!
>   Good beyond all others!

Source of happiness,
incomprehensible good, inestimable good!
Beauty surpassing all beauty,
wisdom beyond all wisdom, Wisdom itself.
You are the bread of angels.
In the ardour of Love,
you give Yourself to man.
You are the vestment which covers all nudity,
the nourishment whose sweetness
rejoices all who hunger.
For You are sweet
without the slightest shadow of bitterness.

O eternal trinity,
show me the way of supreme perfection,
that I may serve You in the light
and not in the darkness.
May I be a mirror of pure and holy life,
renouncing this miserable existence,
where so far I have served you in darkness.

Reclothe me, Eternal Trinity.
Reclothe me with Yourself,
so that I may pass this mortal life
in true obedience,
and in the light of that holy faith
with which You have flooded my soul.

St. Catherine of Siena

2. Communion and our Supernatural Vocation

Communion makes us enter into this mystery of our predestination and sanctification. When we receive Communion, the whole of this mystery passes into us to remain there. The Father is in us in order to communicate His thought and to reveal to us His Word; the Holy Spirit is in us to remain there. And if our fervour corresponds to God's Will, each Communion enlightened by our Faith creates a more intimate communication in the interior of our soul. It makes in us a new resemblance to Jesus, engraved by the Holy Spirit.

We have all been "made to drink of one Spirit" (1 Corinthians 12:13). Communion, in fact, gives us not only the flesh of Jesus, but also His Spirit. It flows into us like a most pure blood, doing for our souls what blood does for our bodies. The Holy Spirit is the source of life. He directed the human nature in Jesus from the first day of His life to the last, inspiring His thought and His love. In the same way, He makes Himself our

Master too, presiding over the supernatural transformation in us. There is the same spirit of Life in Jesus
and in the communicant; there is the same principle
of activity. Provided that the communicant is docile
to His inspirations, there will soon be a perfect assimi-
lation. For the same grace should produce the same
virtues; the same Spirit should enkindle the same acts.
For this reason, we find that the saints acquire such a
resemblance to Jesus that they make with Him one
single heart and soul. They see all things as Jesus would
see them. They have the same desires, the same will,
the same love. *Cor Pauli, cor Christi,* said St. John
Chrysostom: the heart of Paul is the heart of Christ.
Has not the Apostle also said himself, "I live—now not
I, but Christ lives in me" (Gal 2:30)? "Christ takes the
place of my soul," said St. Macaire. Or, as St. Catherine of Genoa puts it, "I have neither heart nor soul.
My heart and soul are those of Jesus Christ."

In the case of St. Catherine of Siena, this mystery of
transformation took place in circumstances which
manifested the singular tenderness of Our Lord.
"One day," recounts Blessed Raymond, "she was repeating fervently the prophet's words, 'Create a clean
heart in me, O Lord, and renew a right spirit within
me' (Psalm 51:10). She asked Our Lord to take away
her heart and her own will. Then she thought she saw
her eternal Spouse come to her as usual. But, He
opened the left side, took her heart, and departed.
The impression left by this vision was so vivid that St.
Catherine told her confessor that she no longer
seemed to have a heart in her body. . . . Some
time afterwards, Our Lord appeared to her bearing
in His sacred Hands a shining human heart. He ap-
proached, opened her left side again, and inserted

there the heart He had held in His hands. 'My beloved daughter,' He said, 'the other day I removed
your heart. Thus, I have now replaced it with my own,
which will make you live eternally.' "

An analogous incident is narrated in the life of St.
Margaret Mary. "The Friday of the Octave of Corpus
Christi," she tells us, "Jesus said to me after Communion, 'My daughter, I have come to you to substitute
My Soul for yours, My heart and My spirit in place of
yours, so that you may henceforth love only by and
for Me.' This grace had such effect that nothing has
subsequently been able to trouble the peace of my
soul, and my heart has no power except to love God
alone. . . ."

This is what Communion achieves: a fusion of heart
and soul. It is true that both these incidents narrated
just now contain facts bordering on the miraculous.
However, leaving these to the side, Communion
should produce in us a similar transformation. Our
aim should be to lose our own proper life and substitute for it the life of Christ, Who declared, "As I live by
the Father, so He who eats Me shall live because of
Me" (John 6:58). In sum: Communion has but one
end: to make us other Christs, other sons of God.

> O all powerful and eternal Trinity! O sweet and
> ineffable love, who would not be inflamed by
> such charity? What heart could refuse spending
> all for You?

> O abyss of charity! You are so intensely attached
> to Your creatures that it would almost seem You
> cannot live without them! Yes, you are God. You
> have no need of us. Since you are unchangeable,
> our well-being adds nothing to Your greatness.

Our wickedness causes You no harm, since You are the sovereign and eternal Goodness. What inspires you with so much compassion? It is love. For, You have no obligation towards us, no need for us. What, then, O infinite God, draws You to me, such an insignificant creature? Nothing other than *Yourself*, fire of Love. Love alone has always impelled, and still impells, Your tenderness towards Your creatures, filling them with infinite graces and priceless gifts. O supreme benevolence, You alone are supremely Good! You have given us the Word, Your Son, to live with us, in touch with such corruption and such darkness. What is the cause of this Gift? Love! For, You loved us before we even existed. . . .

O eternal Magnificence! O immense goodness! You abased yourself. You became little, so that man might become great. Wherever I turn, I find only the abyss and fire of Your love.

St. Catherine of Siena

B. The Glory of the Most Holy Trinity

1. The Supreme End of Creation

We can go still further in the knowledge of our supernatural vocation and ask why God wished that we should become the adopted sons of Jesus Christ.

Certainly, it is for our happiness. As gratuitous as it is immense, His love was not content with drawing us from nothing. He wished also to make us happy, to carry us even to the summit of happiness. This He would do by granting that unheard-of gift, a participation of His nature and a communication of His life.

However, the creature's good cannot be the final purpose of the divine work. Rather, this final goal is the magnificent manifestation of the divine attributes, particularly God's goodness, and the perfect glorification of the Holy Trinity.

By making me happy, God wished to glory Himself. He wishes to be glorified in my happiness.

Ultimately, it is for Himself and for His glory that God has made us His adopted children. Our divine sonship then can just be completed in the love and praise of God. . . . (Eph 1:11, 12). For God, because He is God, "has made everything for its purpose" (Proverbs 16:4). Thus, it is essential that all beings, and our own happiness, be referred to God and pay Him homage.

To glorify God is the essential and primary work of the creature as long as it exists. Everything should be dominated by that fact. It is "the justice" for which we should "hunger and thirst" (Matthew 5:6), as Jesus says in the Beatitudes. To glorify God was both the main cause of the Incarnation and the principal work of the Man Jesus during His life, as well as now in the Blessed Sacrament. He came to save us. But, He came even more to adore and praise His Father. He came to make us happy. But, above all, He was meant to fulfill those duties of religion for which God had waited from the creation of the world. Christ's internal life was an incessant adoration. If He worked, preached, performed miracles, suffered, and died, it was all for the glory of His Father. He was burning with the desire to give Him glory, as though through an interior flame. And this flame consumed Him and never allowed His soul to rest in its thirst for justice and love.

"I have a baptism to be baptized with. And How I am constrained until it be accomplished!" (Luke 12:50). This baptism was the outpouring of blood which would restore to God the glory of the Creation.

"I have earnestly desired to eat this Passover with you before I suffer" (Luke 22:15). This passover was the offering of the Host— of Himself—as a sacrifice of glory.

"I thirst" (John 19:28), He said at the moment of His death. This thirst was the inexpressible need of His heart to witness His love for His Father. It was a thirst which the sacrifice of Calvary could not assuage. For He instituted the Eucharist to renew the outpouring of His blood, to universalize it, and to prolong it throughout the centuries.

Christ's life and death had an aim which governed all His actions. This was, in the first place, to give God the most complete homage He could receive. Secondly, it was to raise up in the world souls who would unite themselves to His love and sacrifice, giving glory with Him and thus being "the true worshipers (who) will worship the Father in spirit and truth, for such the Father seeks to worship Him. . . ." (John 4:23).

> Blessed be the God and Father of our Lord Jesus Christ, who has blessed us in Christ with every spiritual blessing in the heavenly places. . . .
>
> He destined us in love to be His sons through Jesus Christ, according to the purpose of His will, to the praise of His glorious grace which He freely bestowed on us in the Beloved. . . .
>
> In Him, according to the purpose of Him who accomplishes all things according to the counsel of His will, we who first hoped in Christ have been destined and appointed to live for the praise of His glory. . . .
>
> For this reason, I bow my knees before the Father, from whom every family in heaven and on earth is named, that, according to the riches of his glory He may grant you to be strengthened with might through His Spirit in the inner man, and that Christ may dwell in your hearts through faith; that you, being rooted and grounded in love, may have power to comprehend with all the saints what is the breadth and length and height

and depth, and to know the love of Christ which surpasses knowledge, that you may be filled with all the fulness of God.

Now to Him who by the power at work within us is able to do far more abundantly than all we ask or think, to Him be glory in the Church and in Christ Jesus to all generations, for ever and ever.

Amen.

Ephesians 1:3, 5, 6, 11, 12; 3:14-21

2. The Unique Liturgy

Finally, Christ came amongst us in order to accomplish a work of praise—a liturgical work.

He accomplishes it still. For, as the Word Incarnate, Jesus is priest, "the apostle and high priest of our confession" (Hebrews 3:1).

He will accomplish it eternally. For the priesthood was His fundamental state, that which was essential in Him, "He has an everlasting priesthood" (cf Hebrews 7:14). The Father said of Him, "You are a priest forever. . . " (Psalm 110:4).

Thus we see Him, both in heaven and on earth, presiding at the unique liturgy. In one of the most sublime visions of the Apocalypse, St. John shows us our Pontiff exercising His priesthood in the vast assembly of the elect, in the center of the redeemed creation, and in the midst of the throne—even where God is seated. The sevenfold spirit rests on Him and inspires His priesthood. He is upright as one who sacrifices. He is immolated as the universal victim. He gives glory to Him "Who was, Who is, and Who is to come"

(Apocalypse 4:8). And all those who live in Heaven unite themselves to the Lamb to give homage to Him for whom the Lamb sacrifices Himself. "Worthy art thou, our Lord and God, to receive glory and honor and power, for thou didst create all things . . . Holy, Holy, Holy is the Lord God Almighty . . ." (Apocalypse 4:11, 8).

They adore, prostrate themselves, and cast their crowns before the throne to testify that their victory and glory come from the Saviour alone. But, the elect also turn themselves towards the Lamb, who receives the praise which is His due. While He exercises His supreme priesthood, they prostrate themselves before Him. And, with one accord, they intone the new canticle of all the redeemed:

> Worthy is the Lamb who was slain to receive power and wealth and wisdom and might and honor and glory and blessing . . . !
>
> Apocalypse 5:12

These are the grand lines of the liturgy which develops in all its splendour in the heavens under the Presidency of Jesus, the universal Pontiff, and through the breath of the Holy Spirit "by whom the Lamb offered Himself without blemish to God" (cf Hebrews 9:14). But it is exactly the same liturgy which is produced amongst us at the Altar. It is the same priest, the same Victim, the same immolation, and the same aim to be attained. It is only the exterior form which differs: the Church triumphant celebrates the Sacrifice unveiled, while the Church militant celebrates it in faith. But there is only one Liturgy. Every hour a sanctified hymn of praise mounts from the whole world towards the throne of the Most High. The purpose of this is to bless, exalt, and glorify the Lamb who sacrifices Himself. There are innumerable voices from the immense multitude of the redeemed on earth and in heaven. But all these voices form one magnificent chorus and have a single object of praise. Together, they celebrate the unique liturgy. The reason that Jesus offered His sacrifice on Calvary and prolongs it perpetually in the Eucharist is in order that the praise of glory may continually ascend towards God.

Such is also the final goal of Communion.

Jesus desires that the liturgy, the praise which unfolds itself before the throne of God as perfectly united with that on the altar, shall be reproduced in the soul of the communicant.

He comes into us to impel us to enter into that great movement of praise of which He is the Chief and the Pontiff. One day He said to St. Margaret Mary, "I come to baptize you as the supreme Sacrificer." Every baptized person is a consecrated temple, a place destined for the service of praise. "For God's temple is holy, and that temple you are. . . " (1 Corinthians 3: 17). In this temple abides the all-powerful God, the blessed Trinity, to whom sacrifice is offered, "If any man love Me, My Father and I will love him. And we will come to him and make our home with him" (John 14:23).

At Holy Communion, the victim is introduced. The Lamb sacrifices Himself anew. He comes to offer Himself and unite His Sacrifice to the soul that receives Him. For, He wishes that, with Him, we "present our bodies as a living sacrifice, holy and acceptable to God . . ." (Romans 12:1). "The Christian soul," said Origen, "is a permanent altar where the sacrifice perpetuates itself day and night." This sacrifice should not be a passing incident, but rather a permanent state.

For the Lamb who was sacrificed lives on in us even after the dissolution of the bread and the wine. This is in accord with the promise He made, that "through Him we might continually offer up a sacrifice of praise to God—that is, the fruit of lips acknowledging His name" (Hebrews 13:15). Communion allows the soul to celebrate in its sanctuary the sacrifice which the Church triumphant and the Church militant never cease offering to God. The same victim offers Himself there to the same God for the same praise.

Nothing is lacking, "neither the incense, nor the harmony of harps, in that celebrated vision of St. John. The soul's prayer lifts itself up around the sacrifice as a fragrance of sweetness. It says to the Lord that the spouse goes up "Like a column of smoke, perfumed with myrrh and frankincense" (cf Song of Solomon 3:6).

The "sound of the harps" is made up of the harmony of our acts of love. It flows from all those desires, all those varying affections, which pour forth from the heart inspired by the Spirit. A sublime harmony it is—a true echo of the *New Canticle* of the elect. At such a moment, all the powers of soul and body, like the chords of a lyre, are harmonized by purity and penitence.

"Then," said the Heavenly Father to St. Catherine of Siena, "that soul chants a beautiful song, accompanying it on an instrument. And the cords of this instrument have been so well-fashioned by prudence that they form together a holy harmony to the glory and honour of My name. In the case of the great chords, this harmony is produced by the powers of the soul; the smaller chords are produced by the sense of the body. All My saints have captured souls with these harmonies. The first ever to sound them was My well-beloved Word, when clothed with your humanity and united to My divinity. He then played the harmony on the Cross, an ineffable strain that won the love of the human race."

Thus, the same eternal liturgy is celebrated in heaven, on the altar, and in the soul.

To the extent that this praise develops in us, our sanctification advances. When the soul, sustained by perfect love united with intelligence and love to the sacrifice of the Lamb, reaches a certain stage, it has arrived at perfection on this earth. This stage is one in which the soul is not deterred by anything from its task of praise, and when it celebrates that interior worship unceasingly. It lives in the shadows of faith as the blessed do in the eternal vision. And its interior life becomes, said St. Albert the Great, "the prelude and commencement of the life of heaven."

O Holy Trinity,
from whose depths flow forth
in eternal splendour the living divinity,
Love and Wisdom.

O Father, unique source of power:
You who are essential Wisdom,
in Whom goodness wells up unceasingly,
Whose love is ardent as the fire,
Whose holiness is impelled to extend itself
to created beings,
Whose goodness displays itself in all creation,
    to You be praise, honour, and glory.
    To You thanksgiving, power, and light.

This is the fervent desire of my heart.

O Word, tall cedar of Lebanon,
Who in supreme majesty stretched the boughs
of Your divinity above the Cherubim. . . .

yet, it pleased You to descend to the depths
of this vale of tears and seek a humble stem
of hyssop to unite to Yourself by a firm bond,
making it Your spouse in infinite love.

O Holy Spirit. God of Love,
the essential link by love of the Blessed Trinity,
You repose and find delight among the children
of men in holy chastity,
by which Your strength and Your example
flourish here like a rose amongst thorns.

Holy Spirit! Love, Love!
Tell me what road leads to that delightful above.
Tell me where I shall find the path of life
leading to those meadows fertilized
by divine dew, that thirsting souls
may slake their thirst.

O Love, You alone know the road that leads
to life and truth.
In You is accomplished that alliance
full of delights which unites the Persons
of the Holy Trinity.
By You, O Holy Spirit, are poured out on us
the most precious gifts.
From You proceed those fertilized seeds
which produce life-giving fruits.
From You flows the sweet honey of those delights
which are concerned only with God.
By You there descend on us
those irrigating streams of divine blessing,

those precious gifts of the Spirit—
so rare, alas!, in our land.

O Son of God. Love! Love!
Prepare for me the route that leads to You, the path
of love.
Draw me to yourself with chaste affection,
so that I may follow wherever You lead,
even to those heights where you reign
and command in the soverign majesty of Your
divine essence,
to that abode where You bestow
the treasures of Your affection....

While I wait, O Jesus, O Love, in this vale of misery,
keep me in the shadow of Your love.
And after the tedium of this exile,
preserving me from all stain,
conduct and make me enter your sanctuary,
giving me a place in the ranks of that virginal
multitude.

There I shall quench my thirst at the living waters
of Your divine tenderness.
There I shall be sated in the joy
of Your sweet love.

Amen! Amen!
May such be the cry
of every being....

St. Gertrude